⚮ A ⚮
GIFT BOOK
Of
Teddy Bears

A GIFT BOOK
Of
Teddy Bears

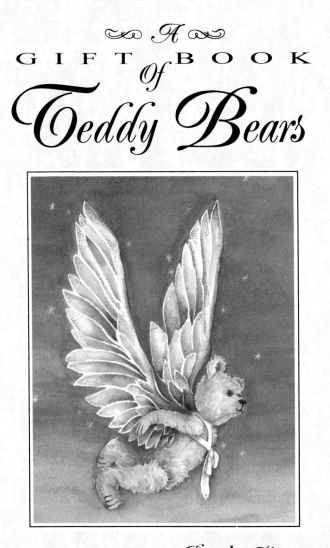

ILLUSTRATED BY *Rosalie Upton*

CRESCENT BOOKS
NEW YORK • AVENEL

Contents

These jolly little Teddy Bears,
Who always love to play,
When hugged by little boys and girls,
They'll scare all gloom away.

The Teddy Bear is Born

The wonder is that the
Teddy Bear should have arrived
so late, for to us the cuddly
creature seems timeless.
Yet, as will be revealed,
the Teddy is really a child of
the twentieth century...

The Bear from Mississippi

On 14 November 1902, President Theodore Roosevelt of the United States was in the middle of settling a boundary dispute in the South when he was taken on a hunting expedition. "Teddy" Roosevelt was a keen hunter, but the story goes that on this occasion the animal they tracked down was only a small, helpless cub. The president spied him, took aim with his rifle, but did not fire. The newspapers took up the tale, and America smiled over the incident and their president's soft heart.

Cartoonist Clifford K. Berryman of the *Washington Evening Star* had fun depicting Roosevelt "Drawing the Line in Mississippi", and his image of this first "Teddy" bear won over America. In the following months, Teddy Bears became the cutest, most cuddly, most wanted creatures in every home. The president, who admired bears both in the wild and on the toyshelf, had accidentally started a new craze.

Furry Friends

I n the nineteenth century in Germany there lived a toymaker named Margarete Steiff. A childhood disease had left her crippled, but with her sister's help she sewed for a living. Her first success as a toymaker was with a felt elephant made into a pincushion, and by 1893 she was exhibiting a range of toy animals at the Leipzig Fair. Her nephew Richard first thought of the idea of a large bear with movable head and joints, made of mohair. Another nephew, Paul, tried to sell these bears, but it was not until the Leipzig Fair of 1903 that success really came for the Steiff factory. The first Steiff bear was known as "Friend Petz", but these popular furry toys began to be imported into the American market, and soon became known as Teddy Bears to suit the new craze. The

 Steiff bears always carried a nickel button in one ear, with the symbol of Margarete's original toy elephant.

These delightful Bears show the true Steiff characteristics,
and are drawn from furry originals.

The Ideal Toy

Morris Michtom laid claim to being the first significant manufacturer of Teddy Bears in the United States. A Russian immigrant, he and his wife ran a small candy store in Brooklyn, and decided to sell Teddies as well, made from brown plush material with movable limbs and button eyes.

Eventually the new furry bears were a familiar sight in toyshop windows, and the Michtoms went on to found the Ideal Toy Corporation, which is still a major manufacturer.

Children today can long for a Teddy as fervently as they did in the early years of the century. It is surprising how many adults also elect the Teddy as the ideal companion throughout their lives.

The Bear in Britain

While Teddies were becoming the darlings of American homes, it so happened that England's Prince of Wales, the future Edward VII, was just cuddly and rounded enough to put one in mind of a portly Teddy Bear. Indeed, on a visit to the London Zoo in 1880, he himself had been lost in admiration for a furry koala, which everyone in those days thought of as a bear. To this day, toy koalas in Australia are known as "Teddy".

It was A.A. Milne who, in the nicest possible way, pointed out that the stout tummy which most self-respecting Teddies possess was shared by England's affable monarch, and the picture of Edward Bear admiring himself in a mirror, and dreaming of royal feasts, pomp and circumstance, is familiar to most British readers.

There is always something regal about a Teddy Bear: no matter how we treat our toy, he has his own dignity, his own secret life.

The Bear in Mythology

In the old, old stories,
bears were as close to us as
our parents, brothers and sisters,
and even a lover
could mysteriously slip
into a bear skin when
the gods willed ...

The Mighty Yu

Mountains and rivers, the haunts of bears, are constant themes in Chinese legends and art. When the earth was young, so they say, there lived a wonderful character, Yu. At the time of the great flood he used magic soil to build up mountains in the four corners of the world, so that they towered above the waters and steadied the earth with their weight. Later he achieved many miracles, directing watercourses on their way to the sea.

During each colossal labour, Yu took the shape of a yellow bear. His greatest feat was to remove Mount Hua from the path of the Yellow River. Gathering his huge strength, Yu pushed with his four paws and split the high mountain in half: the marks of his claws can be seen in the rock to this day.

At thirty, Yu married a woman from T'u-shan in the south, but never let her see his magical shape. Each time he was ready for her to bring him food, he beat a small drum and became her husband again. One day at work he let one rock fall against another, and at this drumlike sound his wife appeared. Terrified of the giant bear, she ran screaming away. Just as Yu caught up with her, she turned into a rock.

Restored to his own form, Yu pleaded with her to reappear, but for nine months she refused, until the day when the rock opened and their son K'i emerged, destined to become King of Hsia after his father.

Atalanta and the Mother Bear

G reek legend tells of a baby girl named Atalanta, whose father was so angry at not having a son that he had her taken up Mount Parthenion in Arcadia, and left to the elements.

A mother bear took pity on the tiny child and reared her with her own cubs, and for many years Atalanta lived surrounded by playful companions, under the protection of her strong, fierce mother. Perhaps she fell in love for ever with the outdoors, or perhaps the rough ways of the bear cubs stayed with her — whatever the reason, although she was later brought up by humans, Atalanta refused both house and husband, and spent her days running wild, hunting with her bow and spear.

Many were the suitors for her hand, but Atalanta challenged each to a foot race, then felled him with her spear as he ran ... until the day when the beautiful youth Melanion tricked her by dropping golden apples in her path, then winning the race when she stooped to pick them up.

An oracle had foretold that Atalanta would be changed into an animal if ever she married, but the bold girl was in love with Melanion, and accepted him with joy. So blissful

were the lovers that one day they forgot themselves and gave
way to their desire in a sacred temple. At this crime, the great
god Zeus struck out in anger and turned the couple into lions.
Thus Atalanta lived out her days as she had begun, with the
woods for her home, and at night a bed of soft leaves and a
roof of stars.

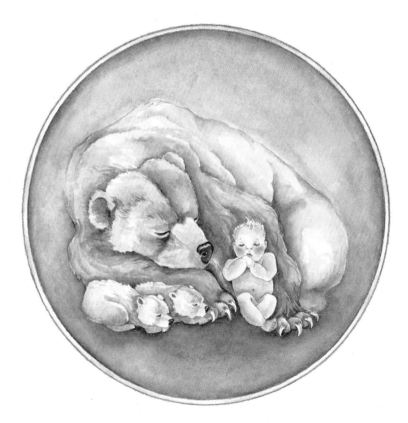

Snow White and Rose Red

Two sisters once lived in a cottage in a wood, where their mother grew two rose bushes, a white one for beautiful Snow White and a crimson one for lovely Rose Red. One midwinter they took pity on a bear that begged for shelter, and every night it slept by their fire. In spring when their gentle friend departed, it tore its coat on the door, and the girls were puzzled to see gold shining beneath its fur.

Three times that summer Snow White and Rose Red came to the rescue of a greedy dwarf, who gave them nothing in return, though he had hordes of gold and jewels hidden in the forest. One day, just after they had saved the dwarf from a mighty eagle, the bear came upon the scene. The dwarf turned on the beast in fury, but with one cuff of its paw the bear silenced him for ever. Afraid, the girls turned away, but a sweet voice called them back: the rough bearskin had fallen to reveal a handsome prince, who had suffered all winter long under the dwarf's spell.

Snow White married the prince, Rose Red married his brother, and the rose bushes bloom still in the deep wood where first they met.

Jakob & Wilhelm Grimm

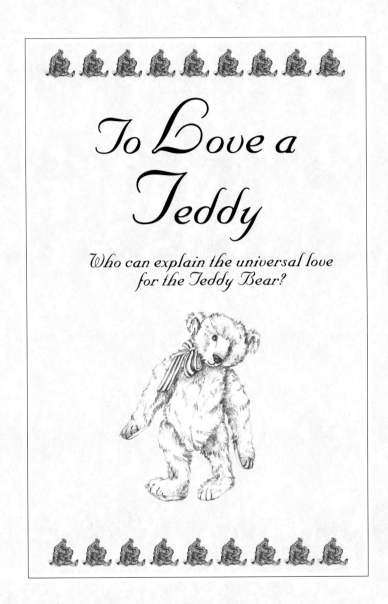

To Love a Teddy

Who can explain the universal love for the Teddy Bear?

Arctophilia

An arctophile is someone who loves Teddies, especially one who collects them. Antique Teddies are bankable items, and very rare ones will fetch high prices at auction. There are people with rooms or houses full of them, who are still ready to pay thousands for yet another "treasure".

There is a great disparity between the fleeting pleasure these expensive Teddies give, and the world of joy that opens up when a child receives its first Teddy, one that may turn into a lifelong friend. A worn scrap of cloth with a button nose may figure more largely in a child's heart and imagination than all his or her other toys put together.

The Teddy Bear has its own value — and it has nothing to do with money.

The Teddy Bear People

They are all over the globe, they may have large collections or just a single bear, they hold rallies and Teddy Bears' picnics, they belong to one of several worldwide clubs, they may even write books on Teddies — all these people believe there is something special about the Teddy Bear.

Most agree that it is the Bear's serene air of acceptance, its way of listening to one's problems and staying calm in crises, that is so endearing. Many people have made great efforts to extend this benefit to others: Colonel Robert Henderson, the great Scottish collector; actor/author Peter Bull in England — and Russell A. McLean, "The Teddy Bear Man" of Lima, Ohio, in the USA.

Russell McLean was convinced that being given a Teddy would cheer up every child that was admitted to hospital in his home town, and he began a campaign, asking the public to send in their sales tax stamps to buy the toys. He achieved his aim: ever since, no child at Lima hospital has missed out on a Teddy Bear. Countless true stories prove that children in pain or fear are comforted by having a bear to hold. Before his death in 1969 The Teddy Bear Man had the joy of presenting Teddy number 50,000.

Bear Psychology

P sychologists have no trouble explaining the tie that binds a Teddy Bear to one who adores him. His animal shape, they say, reflects the archetypal images already in the unconscious, and stirs our imagination. We know instinctively the powerful fearsome aspect of the bear — like the hero Yu, strong enough to split mountains. At the same time, the warm softness of the Bear's fur, his cuddly size and his wordless comprehension of our needs confirm other images in our consciousness — of friendliness, affection and love.

Parents have no trouble understanding the Teddy's appeal, either, for they see these two aspects at work: a child's Teddy Bear is at once the alter ego, and the comforter. How often children will claim that Teddy has said or done things that express the child's own deep adventurous desires: the urge to say disobliging things about a grown-up, or to leap up from the ground and fly away, as one does in dreams. Then, when bedtime comes, Teddy is the soft, furry companion who keeps loneliness at bay.

Teddies do not need to be new or handsome — they just need to be there.

The Literary Bear

*Many artists and writers
who take the Teddy Bear for a theme
find ways to express that fierce,
pure love which belongs only
to childhood …*

Three Cheers for Pooh

The world first met Winnie-the-Pooh when he came downstairs, bump, bump, bump, on the back of his head, behind Christopher Robin. Children have a way of turning things upside down, and A.A. Milne had a wonderful way of understanding them. By rights Christopher Robin's long-suffering toy should have been called Edward Bear, but in Chapter One of his endlessly delightful stories we learn that the name is Winnie-the-Pooh. And that's that. When pushed for an explanation, Christopher Robin replies scornfully, "Don't you know what *ther* means?"

Pooh lives in the woods where the little boy walks every day, but he is also Christopher Robin's very own bear. He has a busy life and friends, and adventures all his own, and at the same time he is always at hand to be talked to, dragged into escapades, bossed about and admonished: "Silly old bear!"

Thanks to A.A. Milne's wit and imagination, and E.H. Shepard's artistry, Pooh now belongs to us all, and no one will ever take his place.

Rupert and the Secret Paths

No Bear has ever been more blithely adventurous than Rupert, nor had a more obliging Mummy and Daddy. On the very brink of danger, he just tells them, "I'm waiting to see if a certain thing's going to happen. Please don't ask me what. It's terribly secret, but I'll tell you someday."

They never do ask, and the adventure always happens. The deceptively safe village of Nutwood, with its meadows, woods and Common, is alive with magic and mystery, and any hedgerow may hide a new path that only Rupert can discover.

This little bear is every child's dream of daring and freedom: he climbs, he digs, he explores far afield, goes out in all weathers, creeps outside at night with a torch — and is repaid for this boldness by breathtaking rides to castles in the clouds, and the promise of tea and buns when he returns home, jaunty and unscathed.

The fact that Rupert takes to the air so often is partly explained by the fact that Mary Tourtel, who created him for the *Daily Express* in 1920, was herself an aviator and adventurer. She illustrated his exploits until 1935, then Alfred Bestall took him up for another thirty years. A team of artists now produces the Rupert comic-strip and this famous Teddy Bear continues on his intrepid way.

The Bear in Boots

T he germ of an idea which later became Paddington occurred to Michael Bond on Christmas Eve in 1956, when he was doing some late shopping, and noticed a Teddy Bear sitting alone on a shelf. He bought him at once, and two years later he saw the first Paddington book launched.

"He's not a cuddly bear," says Michael Bond. "He's a bear for standing up in a corner. That's why he wears Wellington boots."

There is something gruff and determined about Paddington, perhaps a little of true bearishness — but at the same time there is an endearing quality, a hint of dependence that makes one want to pick him up, even if cuddling is frowned upon. His famous label, *PLEASE LOOK AFTER THIS BEAR*, is after all rather a give-away.

A Teddy with a Purpose

Smokey Bear toys are available all over the United States and his face is known to millions. A tireless promoter, he appears in newspapers and magazines across the whole country. He is always on the campaign trail, fighting for a single cause — the preservation of America's forests from the danger of fire.

Smokey is a protector, and his clear message encourages children to be protectors also, by becoming Junior Forest Rangers and understanding the value of the natural environment and its countless families of creatures, all dependent on one another.

In his way, Smokey is an inheritor of that instinct for mutual survival shown by Teddy Roosevelt when he refused to shoot the bear in the Mississippi woods.

Aloysius

I n a story where most of the characters are intent on grabbing and holding onto their little bits of England, Sebastian Flyte, the well-born young exquisite in *Brideshead Revisited* (the novel by Evelyn Waugh) lives by different impulses. He is a student at Oxford, but he thinks more of his Teddy Bear, Aloysius, than he does of his studies. Faithful, understanding, petted and scolded by turns, Aloysius goes everywhere with Sebastian, riding in his open-seater Morris Cowley, enjoying a holiday with him in Italy and later travelling further abroad with his young master.

Just as Sebastian is both spoiled and strangely neglected, so is Aloysius: he has his own ivory-backed hairbrush, with "Aloysius" engraved on it, but the forgetful Sebastian is still capable of leaving him in a cab one night on the way home to college.

In the end, however, Aloysius is really just like other Teddies: mistreated sometimes, but nonetheless adored.

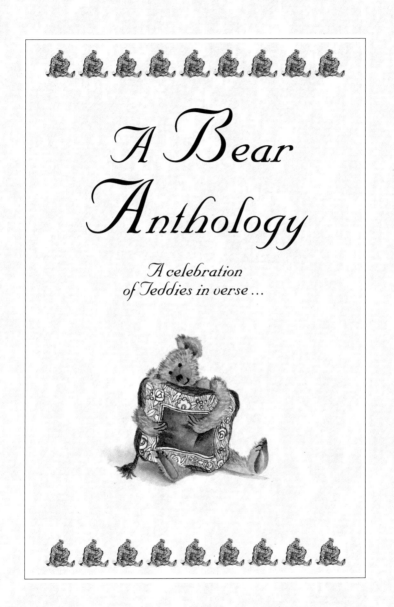

A Bear
Anthology

A celebration
of Teddies in verse ...

Night Bears

BY WILMA HORSBRUGH

Three little bears
From nowhere in particular,
nowhere at all,
Came up the stairs
And climbed the perpendicular,
climbed the perpendicular,
nursery wall.

They sat upon the ceiling
And sang with all their might
Songs so full of feeling
They lasted half the night.

A funny thing it seemed
For little bears to do.
I think I must have dreamed
Those little bears, don't you?

For when the songs were ended
Then down the walls they slid,
And when they had descended
Do you know what they did?

Those three little bears
Went nowhere in particular,
    nowhere in particular,
    flat or or perpendicular,
    nowhere at all.

My Teddy Bear

By.Jeffrey S. Forman

*Lines written to celebrate the bear's
seventy - fifth birthday*

H e sits upon his pillowed throne
   A joyous smile upon his face.
And though his ears might seem outgrown
He carries them with pride and grace.

He's never cross or quick to carp
A friend in need he is to me.

When human tongues are mean and sharp
My teddy gives me sympathy.

To him I always bare my soul.
He lifts me when I'm feeling low.
And when I brag and miss my goal
He never says, 'I told you so.'

My friends may titter gleefully
And some may tease, but I don't care.
I hope that I will never be
Too old to love my Teddy bear.

Furry Bear

By A.A. Milne

If I were a bear,
  And a big bear too,
I shouldn't much care
    If it froze or snew;
I shouldn't much mind
    If it snowed or friz—
I'd be all fur-lined
    With a coat like his!

For I'd have fur boots and a brown fur wrap,
And brown fur knickers and a big fur cap,
I'd have a fur muffle-ruff to cover my jaws,
And brown fur mittens on my big brown paws.
With a big brown furry-down up to my head,
I'd sleep all the winter in a big fur bed.

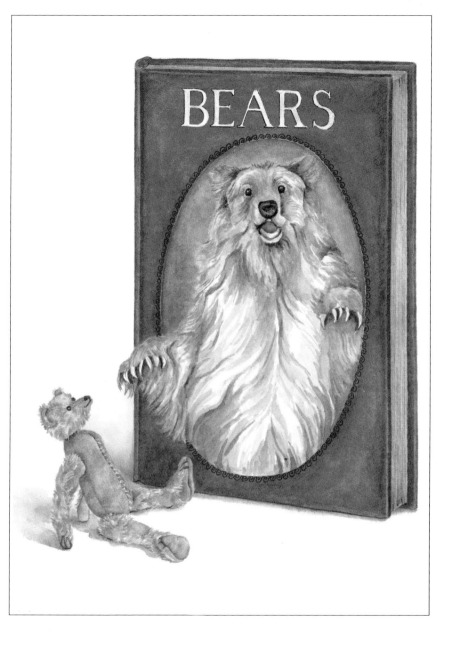

Archie

BY SIR JOHN BETJEMAN

S afe were those evenings in the pre-war world
  When firelight shone on green linoleum;
I heard the church bells hollowing out the sky,
Deep beyond deep, like never-ending stars,
And turned to Archibald, my safe old bear,
Whose woollen eyes looked sad or glad at me,
Whose ample forehead I could wet with tears,
Whose half-moon ears received my confidence,
Who made me laugh, who never let me down.
I used to wait for hours to see him move,
Convinced that he could breathe. One dreadful day
They hid him from me as punishment:
Sometimes the desolation of that loss
Comes back to me and I must go upstairs
To see him in the sawdust, so to speak,
Safe and returned to his idolator.

From *Summoned by Bells*

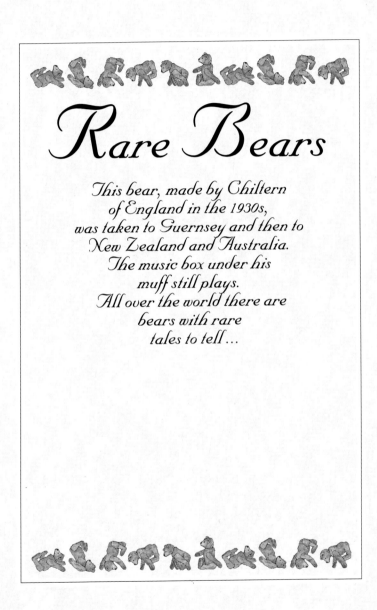

Rare Bears

This bear, made by Chiltern
of England in the 1930s,
was taken to Guernsey and then to
New Zealand and Australia.
The music box under his
muff still plays.
All over the world there are
bears with rare
tales to tell...

Peter the Rarest Bear

From the days when early men fought the great cave bears of the past, these powerful animals have appeared in the old European stories; and in later centuries, the bear was still a popular figure in folk tales. By speaking of him in this way, humans tried to tame this fabulous beast in their minds, so that terror was turned into affection, and fear into trust and love. The gentle, protective bear became legend, and was eventually transformed into a soft, warm creature that even children could hold in their arms.

That is why Peter the Bear is now rare, for he was made in the late 1920s in the town of Neustadt, and he had a fierce face, rolling glass eyes, a wicked tongue, and two rows of pointy wooden teeth. Add to that his realistic growl, which he sometimes came out with while still in his toybox, and no wonder no one wanted to buy him and take him home.

Alas, poor Peter — lonely but not forgotten, he is now the rarest Teddy Bear in the world.

*Fearsome Peter, an unusual antique, is
drawn here from "life".*

The Most Audacious Bear

We do not expect Teddy Bears to be cheeky or pert — somehow they seem too wise and benevolent for that — but there was an early bear who proved himself particularly bold. He belonged to Mr Walter Pelham, who was a young man at Trinity College, Cambridge, when President Roosevelt visited there in 1905.

This audacious bear raised not a murmur of protest when Walter and a friend decided to lower him on a string to confront "Teddy" Roosevelt as he passed beneath their college windows.

Outwardly calm, but no doubt with a thumping heart, Teddy swooped downward on his string and hovered inches from the startled president's nose. The great man stopped, raised his hand, then shook the paw of the little bear.

Only another Teddy could guess what words might have passed between the two on that historic occasion.

The Fastest Bear on Land or Water

M r Woppit first appeared as a character in the children's comic, *Robin,* in 1953. The deputy editor later came to know the great Donald Campbell, and had Mr Woppit made as a present for the famous speedsman. The little bear became his mascot, and travelled in the cockpit of his vehicle whenever he tried for a speed record.

Donald Campbell and Mr Woppit made it in May 1959 on Coniston Water, breaking the world's water speed record at 260.3 miles per hour in the streamlined Bluebird.

In Utah the next year they both came through the fastest car crash in history: Campbell ended up in hospital, but Mr Woppit survived with only a dented nose.

Their great feat was pushing the land speed record to 403 miles per hour.

Then, sadly, Donald Campbell was killed in a crash on Coniston Water in January 1967. Mr Woppit, found floating in the lake, went home to Mrs Campbell, and his flamboyant and faithful racing life came to an end.

Musical Bears

Picnic Day

A family of bears once planned
    A picnic day.
They had their instrumental band,
Were well supplied with tea and cakes
And every article that makes
A splendid time for everyone,
With music, dance and lots of fun
    On picnic day.

They climbed aboard the painted cart
    That picnic day,
And joyfully they made a start,
        All loaded up with every kind
        Of bread and buns that they could find.
    In sunlit fields they spread the food
        And ate and laughed and felt so good
        On picnic day.

The little cubs began to moan
        That picnic day —
The instruments were left at home!
"We have no music!" one cub said,
But then a singer took the lead
And as sweet song rose ever higher
Those bears became a furry choir
        On picnic day.

They chanted far into the dusk
        That picnic day.
The strongest voice sank to a husk,
And with the night they stole away.
The birds now sing for close of day,
The field is dark, the bears have gone
But still their soft song lingers on
        From picnic day.

Teddies, Teddies, Teddies...

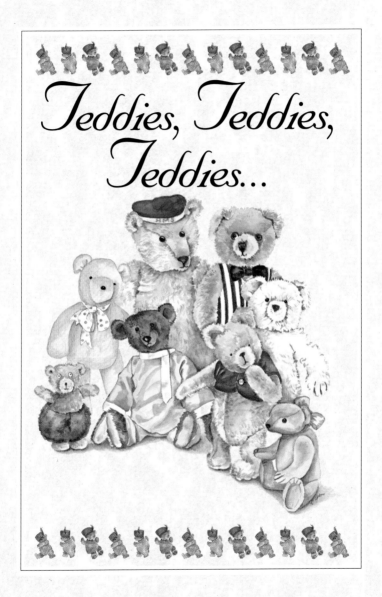

Bears by the Lake

I f you should happen to visit England's beautiful Lake District, you may be honoured by a chance meeting with the newest mysterious inhabitants of the uplands and fells. The dramatic landscapes that were once the inspiration for the poet Wordsworth and the Romantics are the magical home of the Lakeland Bear families.

These are country bears, at one with the hills and valleys, wrapped up against the chill in traditional woollen sweaters and Herdwick tweed, and wearing leather clogs upon their furry feet. Busy as the bees that make the local heather honey, the Lakeland bears are farmers, rangers and foresters, happy in a region green with oaks and chestnuts, and inhabited still by red squirrels.

Some Lakeland bears go backpacking, and should you meet them on a highland track, they may share a crumble of mintcake with you, or lend you a walking stick (very useful if you happen to be like them - 18 inches tall). Then, in the wink of an eyelid, the little creatures will vanish into the mist, leaving behind a hint of Lakeland mystery.

The Amazing Dancing Bear

In Russia once an Empress reigned:
Elizabeth, famed for her jewels and dresses,
  A devotee of fine champagne,
With mischievous eyes, and abundant gold tresses.

  Saint Petersburg one winter was chill:
The Empress flung wide all her windows and doors,
  The Neva flooded over the sill
And froze overnight on the smooth palace floors.

  There never was a party since
Where the beauties, the music or wine could compare;
  Much to the joy of every prince
The delight of the night was a dancing black bear.

  He took to the ice on silver skates,
Pirouetted and whirled with incredible speed,
  He juggled baubles and golden plates,
In all of the dancing the bear took the lead.

  His midnight fur, his eyes so bright
In the colourful throng glittered everywhere
  And no one ever forgot the night
When the Empress invited the dancing bear.

An Indian Love Chant

In the mountains, by the rivers,
Lived the bears of ancient story,
Lived and hunted, loved and married,
Told their cubs of tribal glory.

One bear tale among the many
Sang of Furry Bear and White Dove,
Bears who yearned to be together,
Bears whose parents dimmed their bright love.

Rigid was the parents' honour,
Fatal was the parents' anger:
Never were the two to marry,
Even touching paws spelt danger.

By a wigwam, all in secret,
Furry Bear met little White Dove.
Each in joy and proud defiance
Swore their passion was the right love.

Then they pledged eternal union,
Joined their paws, sped to the river,
Plunged together, kissed, and perished:
So their love goes on for ever.

Teddy Bear Biscuits

A ll you need to begin with is a biscuit cutter in the shape of a Teddy Bear, and a sweet tooth.

∞

INGREDIENTS

125g butter or margarine
60g sugar
3 heaped teaspoons condensed milk
a few drops of vanilla essence
200g flour
1 teaspoon baking powder
1 teaspoon cinnamon
30g dark chocolate chips
1 small egg

∞

METHOD

Cream the butter, sugar and condensed milk, and add the essence.

Add the dry ingredients and chocolate chips.

Add enough of the beaten egg to make a stiff mixture.

Roll out gently on a floured board to 0.5cm thickness

and cut with biscuit cutter.
Place on a cold, greased tray and bake 20 –
minutes at 190°C.

Any small bear will be delighted to help you eat these
biscuits, and without much prompting will finish off the
leftover condensed milk.

"My True Love Hath My Heart ..."

My true love hath my heart, and I have his,
By just exchange one for the other given.
I hold his dear, and mine he cannot miss;
There never was a better bargain driven.
His heart in me keeps me and him in one;
He loves my heart, for once it was his own;
I cherish his, because in me it bides.

SIR PHILIP SIDNEY

Acknowledgements

The publisher is grateful to the following for permission to reproduce copyright material or to represent a copyright image: 39 Reproduced by permission of Lemon, Unna and Durbridge Ltd. © 1992 Paddington & Co., 46 Wilma Horsbrugh: 50 "Furry Bear" by A.A. Milne, published by Methuen Children's Books; 52 "Archie" by John Betjeman, John Murray (Publishers) Ltd. Thanks are also extended to Yvonne Tonnison and The Teddy Bear Shop, Double Bay, Sydney, Australia; and to the Lakeland Bear Co, England.

The publisher has made every effort to trace copyright holders. If we have inadvertently omitted to acknowledge anyone, we should be most grateful if this could be brought to our attention.

First published by Kevin Weldon and Associates Pty Ltd 1992
Reprinted by Lansdowne Publishing Pty Ltd 1993

This 1995 edition published by Crescent Books,
Distributed by Random House Value Publishing, Inc.,
40 Engelhard Avenue, Avenel, New Jersey 07001

Random House
New York • Toronto • London • Sydney • Auckland

©Copyright: Lansdowne Publishing Pty Ltd 1992
©Copyright design: Lansdowne Publishing Pty Ltd 1992

Illustrated by Rosalie Upton
Text by Cheryl A. Hingley
Designed by Denese Cunningham
Printed by Tien Wah Press (Pte) Ltd

A CIP catalog record for this book is available from the Library of Congress
ISBN 0-517-12124-7

PHILOSOPHICAL
REASONING

Also by John Passmore

A Hundred Years of Philosophy
(rev. ed.; Basic Books, 1966)
Hume's Intentions
(Basic Books, 1968)

PHILOSOPHICAL REASONING

JOHN PASSMORE

PROFESSOR OF PHILOSOPHY
AT THE
AUSTRALIAN NATIONAL UNIVERSITY

Basic Books, Inc., Publishers

NEW YORK

Basic Books edition, 1969
© 1961 by John Passmore
Library of Congress Catalog Card Number: 77-93694
Printed in the United States of America

CONTENTS

Preface

PHILOSOPHERS have often enough set out to describe and examine the reasoning of mathematicians, the reasoning of experimental scientists, the reasoning of historians. I have attempted, in the same spirit, to describe and examine the reasoning of philosophers. But in such a way, I hope, as to avoid two common defects of methodological writings: insufficient illustration, and an undue anxiety to assimilate the varieties of rational procedure to a single type—as if, for example, mathematicians never did anything but deduce conclusions from axioms, experimental scientists never reasoned except in the process of testing hypotheses, and historians wholly restricted themselves to the construction of narratives.

Illustration, however, has its difficulties: any interpretation of a great philosopher is likely to provoke controversy. I have sometimes been obliged to ride roughshod over the finer feelings of scholars; I did not wish to interrupt the development of my general theme by defending in detail, or expounding in a less schematic way, the interpretations I have proposed. If this or that example is questioned, another may pass muster; a single illustration would suffice, logically, to make my point, since I am only concerned to show that certain reasoning-procedures do exist and are valid, not to establish their frequency. This is not a work of scholarship, although I have tried not to be unscholarly.

My theme is such that I have been obliged to make *ex parte* pronouncements on a large number of philosophical topics. I have had to go out on a limb in order to survey a broader prospect. If the limb is rotten I must bear the consequences; and I know, at least, that I have not always proved it to be sound. But if I have sometimes been dogmatic, this is not because I would dismiss positions alternative to my own as too contemptible to deserve attention, but rather because I have judged, rightly or wrongly, that direct presentation, rather than close controversy, was in the present case the best method of discussion. For the same reason I have had nothing to say about such works as H. W. Johnstone's *Philosophy and Argument* (1959).

Finally, I have presented the reader with a set of arguments, supposed all of them to be philosophical, rather than with a generalized description of philosophical reasoning. I have for a long time doubted whether such a generalized description is possible even in regard to mathematical arguments—whether we can say anything more than that certain types of argument, themselves various in type because mathematical purposes are also varied, are largely peculiar to mathematics; I am under no obligation, at least, to offer a generalized description in the case of philosophical arguments. I have described a set of reasoning-procedures which have certainly been conspicuous in the history of philosophy; I have examined them critically; I have tried to show that it would be wrong to assimilate them to familiar types of mathematical and experimental reasoning. That is certainly enough for my present purposes; and perhaps it is enough, and all that is possible, absolutely. There are no doubt 'family resemblances' between certain of these reasoning-procedures, resemblances to which I have sometimes drawn attention, but I have not wished to presume that their peculiarities can be summed up in some simple formula. If they can be, so much the better; whether they can be, need not at the outset be decided.

This book grew out of a series of lectures delivered at Brandeis University, during my tenure of the Ziskind Visiting Professorship. It owes a great deal, even where it is critical of them, to the writings of Professor Gilbert Ryle; and even more to his personal encouragement. The lectures of Professor John Anderson, at the University of Sydney, were my first introduction to philosophical reasoning. In part, what I am describing is what he practised, although even that, to say nothing of my more specific conclusions, he might wish to dispute. Dr. Robert Brown forced me to clarify my thought on a number of issues. Mrs. F. Dadd, as departmental secretary, has coped remarkably well with my somewhat idiosyncratic handwriting. Since this book was composed, for the most part, in foreign lands, my wife and daughters were called upon to add secretarial to their other responsibilities—not least the responsibility of bearing patiently with my preoccupation.

JOHN PASSMORE

Institute of Advanced Studies,
    Australian National University,
    Canberra.

Chapter One

THE DISTINCTIVENESS OF PHILOSOPHICAL REASONING

ARE THERE special modes of reasoning, characteristic of philosophy and not to be found, or at least not conspicuously present, outside it? If Hume is right—and his views on this matter still form part of the 'mental furniture' of a great many philosophers—there most certainly are not. In his *Inquiry concerning Human Understanding*, he addresses his readers thus:

'If we take in our hand any volume; of divinity or school metaphysics, for instance; let us ask *Does it contain any abstract reasoning concerning quantity or number?* No. *Does it contain any experimental reasoning concerning matter of fact and existence?* No. Commit it then to the flames; for it can contain nothing but sophistry and illusion.'[1]

According to Hume, then, all valid reasoning is either 'abstract reasoning concerning quantity or number' or 'experimental reasoning concerning matter of fact'—inference, that is, which is founded on our experience of constant conjunction. Only experimental inference, he argues, can lead to the conclusion that such-and-such an entity exists, and experimental inference is always nondemonstrative. 'There is no Being', so he sums up in his *Dialogues Concerning Natural Religion*, 'whose existence is demonstrable' (ed. N. Kemp Smith, p. 189). Since deductive metaphysics attempts to demonstrate the existence of a particular entity, e.g. God, it must be sophistical; were it truly demonstrative, it could issue only in equations, not in existence statements.

This conclusion has been very widely accepted. Every

[1] Par. XII, pt. III. Ed. A. Selby Bigge (Oxford, 2nd ed., 1902), p. 165.

I

young philosopher soon discovers that 'deductive metaphysics' is one of the 'dismissal-phrases', if I may so describe them, of contemporary philosophical controversy. It functions in the same manner as 'crass materialism' or 'sheer empiricism' in the nineteenth century, or 'scholasticism' in Hume's time. If a theory can be thus described, one feels free, at once, to dismiss it from serious consideration. As always happens in these circumstances, the phrase 'deductive metaphysics' has come to be used very loosely; for example, Alexander's *Space, Time and Deity* is often described as 'deductive metaphysics' although it sets out to be purely descriptive—Alexander[1] even says that he has a positive distaste for argument! But if by 'deductive metaphysics' is meant the attempt to deduce the existence of specific kinds of thing from self-evident principles, I should not wish to argue for its reinstatement.

Deductive metaphysics, thus understood, takes one of two forms. The first type sets out from principles which are both self-evident and non-existential and attempts to deduce from these principles alone that such-and-such an entity must exist. Thus the ontological argument attempts to deduce the existence of God from the principle that, as Aquinas puts it, 'that which exists actually and mentally is greater than that which exists only mentally'.[2] Hume's, and the general, objection to this sort of deductive metaphysics is that there is no conceivable way in which an existential conclusion could be deduced from non-existential premises. The second type of deductive metaphysics, seeing the force of this objection, adds a premise which is allegedly both self-evident and existential, e.g. Descartes' 'I exist as a thinking being'. Then the objection is that the metaphysician's existential premises are either not self-evident or else collapse, when subjected to critical examination, into tautologies. This is not an accident—Descartes was not an unskilful metaphysician. No proposition which asserts that

[1] See his 'Some Explanations' (*Mind*, 1921).
[2] *Summa Theologica*, Question 2, Article 1, Obj. 2.

2

something exists can be self-evident, nor can such a proposition be deduced from non-existential premises.

All this granted, however, it by no means follows, as Hume and his followers have thought it did, that every non-sophistical argument is either a causal inference or a mathematical demonstration. Consider the following argument, from the *Enquiry* (par. IV, pt. II) itself:

'We have said that all arguments concerning existence are founded on the relation of cause and effect; that our knowledge of that relation is derived entirely from experience; and that our experimental conclusions proceed upon the supposition that the future will be conformable to the past. To endeavour, therefore [to construct] the proof of this last supposition by probable arguments, or arguments regarding existence, must be evidently going in a circle, and taking that for granted, which is the very point in question' (p. 35).

This is a relatively straightforward example of deductive reasoning. From the set of premises he specifies Hume deduces that *all arguments concerning existence* must be based on the supposition that the future will resemble the past. It then immediately follows that the same is true of *such arguments concerning existence as profess to prove that the future will resemble the past*. In other words, any attempt to justify induction by an appeal to experience is bound to be circular.

This deduction is of great importance for Hume; if it is to be cast into the flames as 'sophistry and illusion' much of the force of the *Enquiry* will be destroyed with it. Yet where is the causal reasoning, where the reference to quantity and number? 'All those pretended syllogistic reasonings, which may be found in every other branch of learning, except the sciences of quantity and number', so Hume tells us (p. 163), are nothing but definitions in disguise. But he certainly would not wish to admit that his own syllogisms are merely definitions. They are not 'demonstrations', as he understands that word—for premises and conclusions *could*

3

be false—but they are not definitions in disguise, either, nor yet are they causal inferences.

No one has ever tried harder than Hume to show that all non-sophistical metaphysical reasoning is, in his sense of the word, 'experimental'; it consists wholly, he argues, in drawing conclusions by causal inference from particular observations about human nature. Yet argument after argument, especially in the *Treatise*—for the *Enquiry*, on the whole, is a summary of conclusions rather than a reasoned case—fails to fulfil Hume's specifications, by being neither concerned with quantity nor causal.

Hume's criticism of the attempt to justify induction by an appeal to experience is a particularly interesting example, in so far as it issues in the conclusion that any such attempt at justification will involve a *petitio principii*. For this is not a *formal* objection; so that even if we extend the range of the mathematical to include formal logic, Hume's argument is still not mathematical. If, when asked to prove that Socrates is mortal, we reply: 'Both Socrates and Plato are mortal, therefore Socrates is mortal' we do not commit a formal fallacy. Indeed, it would be self-contradictory to say of an argument both that it is formally fallacious and that it involves a *petitio*; for that would imply that its conclusion both does and does not follow from its premises.

Nor, when we allege that an argument involves a *petitio*, are we rejecting one of its premises, on experimental grounds, as false. What we are saying, rather, is that the argument *does not constitute a proof*. In this context—the context of empirical inquiry—a 'proof' argues to the truth of a proposition which we do not know to be true by showing that it follows from propositions we already believe to be true; in the case of a *petitio principii*, however, the truth of the premises cannot be more obvious than the truth of the conclusion, seeing that the premise already asserts the conclusion. When Mill said that every syllogism, taken at its face value, involves a *petitio principii* he was not denying

4

that syllogisms are valid, nor was he asserting that their premises are always false; rather, he was making the philosophical point that a syllogism is not, as he puts it, a 'real inference'. This objection depends upon a formal analysis—Mill has to show that the conclusion is in fact already asserted in the premises—but it does not itself make a formal point, for there is no formal objection to asserting the conclusion in a premise. This, indeed, is characteristic of a great many philosophical arguments: they make use of formal analyses without themselves being formal analyses.

One can see why Hume was anxious to deny that there could be forms of reasoning other than the mathematical and the experimental, for this was a rapid way of ruling out deductive metaphysics. If all deductive arguments are mathematical, it at once follows that there can be no deductive metaphysical reasonings. Yet it is quite apparent that there are a great many arguments, inside and outside philosophy, which are neither mathematical reasonings nor causal inferences. Unlike causal inferences, they are not attempts to predict the future or to retrodict the past— more generally, to infer the existence of unexperienced entities; unlike mathematical reasonings, they are not con- cerned with 'quantity and number' or, more broadly, with ordered series. My present argument is a case in point; to reject the view that all valid deductions are mathematical by pointing to a particular non-mathematical deduction is not to engage in causal reasoning. Nor is it to embark upon mathematics, even in the most extended sense of that somewhat elastic word.

We might, however, wish to go further; by asserting not only that there are arguments which are neither mathe- matical nor causal but also that this distinction has not the sort of formal significance which Hume ascribed to it. Hume thought that all scientific inference is, to use the language of a later day, 'inductive'; and that mathematics is uniquely deductive. Consider, however, the process of falsifying a scientific hypothesis. If the hypothesis is true, it is argued, such-and-such must be the case; since it is not the case, either the hypothesis or some conjointly held proposition is false. Whatever our views about scientific method, we can scarcely deny that arguments of this sort play *some* part in science; they are deductive, and yet can properly be described as 'experimental reasonings'. Thus we can say this: the distinction between mathematical and experimental reasoning does not correspond to a wholly formal distinction between two different types of reasoning, induction and deduction (granting, for the sake of argument, that there are inductive inferences at all). On the contrary, experimental reasoning, sometimes or always, is *deductive inference used in a certain way*—used in order to test hypotheses; mathematics is deductive inference used in a different way, to deduce conclusions from axioms, for example. 'If p were true, q would follow', does not say exactly the same thing as 'since p is true, q is true'; and 'if p were true q would follow', where p is a scientific hypothesis and q a particular observation, is different in important respects from 'if p were true, q would follow', where p is a supposition and q an equivalent supposition. Yet although these differences are, for certain purposes, so important, they do not involve a distinction between different types of validity—inductive validity and deductive validity.

Consider now the question from which we set out: 'Are there special modes of reasoning, which are characteristic of philosophy?' It might have been interpreted thus: 'Are there philosophical modes of reasoning, which are neither inductive nor deductive?' To that question, the answer can be given immediately. 'No'. Philosophical reasoning, if it is to be valid at all, must be deductive in its formal structure. But, I am now suggesting, reasoning can be distinctive in a respect other than its formal structure. Testing a hypothesis is very different from constructing an algebraic proof, even if in both cases the reasoning is deductive. The only real question is whether philosophical reasonings have, or can have, peculiarities which are not exhibited either in

6

the typical reasoning-procedures of the experimental scientist, or in the typical reasoning-procedures of the mathematician—peculiarities, perhaps, which are not of any particular interest to the logician but which would make it inappropriate to refer to philosophical reasoning as being either experimental or mathematical. Hume's argument—'any attempt to justify induction by an appeal to experience must take such-and-such a form; any demonstration of that form involves a *petitio*; therefore induction cannot be justified by an appeal to experience'—is certainly deductive, but it neither tests a hypothesis, deduces a conclusion from axioms, nor employs any of the other reasoning-procedures in which experimental scientists or mathematicians ordinarily engage. It tries to show that something cannot be done, but not because (in the scientific manner) it would be inconsistent with some physical law, as a physicist might argue that it is impossible to construct a perpetual motion machine; nor because the supposition that it can be done leads to formal contradiction, like the supposition that a circle can be squared; but rather because any attempt to do it *presumes that it has already been done*. This is one of the most characteristic procedures in philosophy; we shall meet something very similar in our discussion of the infinite regress.

Of course, even if there are peculiarly philosophical arguments it does not follow that the philosopher will be wholly engaged in deploying them. McTaggart thought, as Keeling put it, that 'the technical study of metaphysics is concerned at almost every step, with proving or disproving something' (Introduction to J. M. E. McTaggart: *Philosophical Studies*, p. 14). But in fact this is not so; the philosopher spends a great deal of his time in describing, or classifying, or defining, or analysing, or disproving. He is trying to solve certain problems, and in the attempt to solve problems, proof plays only a limited part.

Nor is the philosopher restricted to the exercise of any particular set of reasoning-procedures. As Karl Popper has emphasized: 'Philosophers are as free as others to use any method in searching for the truth'. Circumstances may arise, circumstances have indeed arisen, in which an experimental scientist will wish to use an argument of the sort we ordinarily identify as 'philosophical'; as when, say, William Harvey criticized his opponents not on the ground that their mathematics were weak or their experimental science inadequate, but because their theories were, he said, empty of content. Similarly a philosopher might find it desirable to construct a proof that is mathematical in character, or to engage in experimental reasoning, or to refer to the experimental reasonings of others, in the course of pursuing some problem which he is trying to solve. Characteristically, however, his arguments are neither mathematical nor experimental.

The arguments of everyday life, of course, are in the same position; we should certainly not wish to describe them as being either experimental or as mathematical. When somebody says: 'You'll be tired if you climb that mountain; you're not a boy any longer', or 'I can't do everything; I've only got two legs', it would be unnatural to describe these arguments as pieces of experimental or mathematical reasoning. But this is not because they are peculiar in form, or unusual in what they set out to show, but solely because their premises and conclusions are not of the sort with which scientists or mathematicians concern themselves. Such arguments refer neither to mathematical formulae nor to physical laws; they simply remind us of a familiar fact of everyday life.

Philosophers, as it happens, need a lot of reminding. Traditionally they assert very wide generalizations referring to a great range of facts—and this applies as much to people who say that 'the meaning is the use' or that 'all philosophical problems arise out of a misunderstanding of our language' as it does to those who try to persuade us that everything is made out of water or is an appearance of the Absolute. A natural way of dealing with the enthusiasm of philosophers is to pull them up with a reminder. A philosopher will say, as Hume does, that to remember something is just to have a vivid perception, and we remind him: 'But to claim to remember is to claim to know that *something happened in the past*'. Now, as Ayer has insisted in his 'Statements about the Past' (*Philosophical Essays*, p. 175), to make this point is not at all to put forward a theory about remembering or about the past. One can go on to ask whether we do in fact ever know that something happened in the past, under what conditions such knowledge can occur, and so on. But the fact remains that it is a tremendously important statement to make, for it brings home the fact that a theory of remembering has to be a theory of our claim to know that such-and-such happened in the past. If the theory describes 'memory' in such terms that we could claim to remember something without claiming that anything happened in the past then it cannot be satisfactory as a theory of memory. And this is true of Hume's theory: for clearly to claim that we are now having a particularly vivid perception is not to claim anything at all about the past.

It is amazing how effective and important these reminders can be. People can be led into saying that 'words are names', quite forgetting that 'or' and 'if' and 'the' are words; or can assert that 'the meaning of a word is the way it is used', quite forgetting that a misuse is not a non-use but a way of using, and it can be extremely important—at a certain stage in human thought—for someone to mention this sort of quite obvious fact. Indeed Wittgenstein was so impressed by the role played by reminders that he asserted that the whole work of the philosopher 'consists in assembling reminders for a particular purpose' (*Philosophical Investigations*, p. 127). This was a natural view for him to take because there has been a special need for reminders in recent years. The prevailing theories at the turn of the century—especially certain types of sense-datum theory and certain types of meaning theory—were particularly vulnerable to criticism by reminding. They claimed to be 'empiricist', but empiricism had turned into a detailed and elaborated theory of perception, moving very far away indeed from anything we should ordinarily describe as 'experience'. Another reason, of course, for the popularity of some such view as that philosophy consists in assembling reminders is that philosophers have been reacting violently against deductive metaphysics; reminding has seemed a particularly useful and appropriately modest sort of thing to do, in contrast with the bolder but emptier ambitions of the traditional metaphysician.

Formally, of course, 'reminding' is parallel to the falsification of a hypothesis; a proposition is rejected on the ground that it would lead to consequences—e.g. that 'the' is a name, or, in the case of Russell's logical atomism, that 'this' is a proper name—which are clearly false. Yet we would be reluctant to describe reminding as an example of experimental reasoning, because, as I said earlier, the facts used in disproof are not ordinarily derived by any special effort of experiment and observation. Let us simply call arguments of this sort 'disproofs by reminder' and recognize that they play an important part in philosophy, although, of course, they can also be used in everyday life or in any branch of science. Anybody can, in a moment of zeal, forget or fail to bring to bear upon the present situation some fact which is perfectly familiar to him. The only thing is that, as compared with other theorists, philosophers are particularly good at forgetting familiar facts, perhaps just because the facts they forget are so familiar that they are never explicitly before the mind as facts. 'One is unable to notice something—because it is always before one's eyes' (*Philosophical Investigations*, p. 129)—or 'before one's eyes' in a certain sense, although not in another sense.[1] For perhaps nobody has ever said to himself that ' "the" is not a name' or that 'in remembering we claim that something has happened in the past' unless he has had occasion to do so as

---

[1] Compare Rousseau: 'Il faut beaucoup de philosophie pour savoir observer une fois ce qu'on voit tous les jours'.

part of the process of 'reminding' in a philosophical disproof. The peculiarity of some philosophical reasonings, then, consists simply in the fact that the premises they employ are of such an apparently trivial and obvious character; one does not need any special training or skill to see that the premises are true. And yet they are not the sort of premises, either, which we ordinarily use in everyday life. They remind us not of something we once knew but have now forgotten, but rather of something we now need to notice but never before have needed to notice.

Another very common philosophical reasoning-procedure is verbal analysis—the detection, for example, of concealed ambiguities. Of course, this can be necessary in other forms of inquiry, too; it is certainly very common in controversies within the social sciences. But so prominent is it in philosophy that verbal discriminations would very commonly be thought of as forming the 'philosophical' part of any scientific argument within which they appear. The use of this technique goes back to relatively early times in philosophy. Plato's distinction in the *Republic* between two meanings of 'interests of the stronger'—what is *really* advantageous to the stronger and what *he believes to be* advantageous to him—is a familiar example. The discussion of 'not-being' in Plato's *Sophist*, where Plato tries to answer Parmenides by distinguishing between 'not-being' in the sense of *not existing at all* and 'not-being' in the sense of *not being so-and-so*, is a more professional example of the same sort of technical device. In the history of philosophy, distinctions of this sort have constantly turned out to be of the first importance; philosophical analyses, in the work of a variety of thinkers, have led to a much closer understanding of such notions as 'necessity', 'freedom', 'law'.

Philosophers, however, have not been interested in the mere fact (considered for its own sake) that words have a variety of meanings; they have not been concerned with, or about, such facts as that 'a table' can mean either an article of furniture or a list of numbers, or that men can die

11

for a cause as well as *from* a cause. They have pursued linguistic analysis—even the most recent exponents of it—only in so far as it throws light upon the traditional problems of philosophy. (As Austin talked about 'if' and 'can', not about 'cliff' and 'scan'.)

Very often, indeed, such verbal analyses have appeared as part of an argument, and an argument which has a specifically philosophical look to it. Consider the hypothesis that 'everyone pursues his own interests'. In rebutting this hypothesis somebody might bring counter-examples, either by reminding us of familiar cases or by referring to experimental facts. He might say 'Some people die for a cause; surely they do not pursue their own interests'; or he might say 'Of twenty rats put in a maze . . .'. There would be nothing peculiarly philosophical about either argument.

But his argument might take a different form, as it does, say, in Rashdall's *Theory of Good and Evil*. It might run something like this: 'The phrase "pursue one's own interests" is ambiguous. If by "pursuing one's own interests" you mean "doing what one is interested in", then, of course, the man who dies for a cause is interested in this cause; if not a tautology, it is at least a trivial proposition that everyone pursues his own interests. But if "pursuing his own interests" means doing something that will bring a person "profit", in the sense of greater possessions, then it is obviously not true that people never act except "in their own interest". So the statement "Everybody pursues his own interests" if interpreted in one way is trivial, if in another is clearly false'.

Similarly, in epistemological controversy, a great deal of the philosopher's time (although perhaps even now not enough of his time) has been taken up in unravelling the ambiguities inherent in the epistemological use of such words as 'experience', 'perception', 'judgement'—ambiguities which make it possible to shift backwards and forwards between 'a perception' in the sense of 'something I perceive' and 'a perception' in the sense of some supposed act of perceiving. The epistemologist may not even notice that a simple-looking sentence like 'I can only be aware of my own perceptions' can be a way of asserting either the bare tautology 'I can perceive only what I perceive' or, on the contrary, the clearly false proposition 'What I perceive is always an act of my own mind'. Indeed, the plausibility of a good deal of epistemological argument depends upon treating 'I can only be aware of my own perceptions' as if it were an obvious truth—as it is on one interpretation of the sentence—and at the same time as a quite striking discovery about the world, as it would be, were it true, on the second interpretation of the sentence. Of course, to point out, simply, that a sentence has two different interpretations, on one of which it is trivial or tautological, on the other non-trivial, is not to say that the non-trivially interpreted sentence is false—it might be true. But, very often, that it is false will be immediately obvious, once we see clearly what it is asserting.

Of recent philosophers, G. E. Moore was especially notable both for his skill in using 'reminding' arguments— he hoped to dispel a great deal of metaphysical fuzz by the simple process of reminding us of what we already know— and for his ability to bring out different interpretations of a sentence, one making it trivial, another making it false. Consider, for example, Moore's discussion of 'Imaginary Objects', as part of a symposium with Ryle and Braith- waite.[1] Ryle had talked about the class of propositions— those in *Pickwick Papers*—which, he said, seem to be about Mr. Pickwick but are not in fact about Mr. Pickwick. And Moore asks: What can possibly be meant by saying that they are not in fact about Mr. Pickwick? One thing Ryle could mean, Moore suggests, is just that nobody called Mr. Pickwick ever existed, in the sense in which Mr. Baldwin existed. A naïve person reading *Pickwick Papers* might imagine it was a history book, not a novel, and to

[1] *Proc. Ar. Soc.*, Supplementary Volume XII (1933).

such a person we might say 'There never has been a Mr. Pickwick'. But if this is what Ryle meant, then, Moore argues, no philosopher has ever supposed otherwise, whereas Ryle obviously thinks he is saying something which is inconsistent with somebody's philosophical views.

A second thing Ryle might have meant is that Mr. Pickwick is not what some philosophers have called 'a logically proper name', and Moore says he would agree with Ryle on this point. But he comments thus: 'It seems to me that in many parts of his paper, particularly in what he says about the meaning of "being real", he utterly confuses this proposition that Dickens was not using "Mr. Pickwick" as "a logically proper name", with the totally different proposition that he was not using "Mr. Pickwick" as a proper name (in the ordinary sense) *for anyone*. This, of course, involves a confusion between two corresponding senses of "about". So far as by "Dickens' proposition was not *about* anyone" Ryle means "Dickens was not using 'Mr. Pickwick' as a logically proper name", he is using "about" in one sense, and is saying something inconsistent with a philosophical view which has been held. So far as he means only "There never existed anyone at whom one could have pointed and said truly 'That is the person Dickens meant by "Mr. Pickwick"'", he is using "about" in a totally different sense, and is saying something that is of no interest for philosophy. But he seems to me to have been quite unaware of the difference between the two.'

Nobody who reads a passage of this sort could doubt that he was reading philosophy, and this not only because it includes the technical expression 'logically proper name'. Such a method of analysis—dealing with an argument by disentangling different senses, and especially by distinguishing the trivial sense from a non-trivial sense—is typically philosophical. Furthermore, one might well be prepared to say that unless a man has the sort of gift Moore displays in this passage he is not a philosopher. That is why Bradley is a philosopher in a sense which, say, a theosophist is not; even if their final conclusions look almost indistinguishable.

Very many of my contemporaries, I suppose, would be willing to agree with me so far. They would willingly admit that 'assembling reminders' is an appropriate philosophical procedure. They might also admit that the construction of analytic dilemmas—'if you mean such-and-such, that is true but trivial; if such-and-such, it is then not trivial, but neither is it obviously true'—is characteristically philosophical. Hume, they would say, was obviously mistaken in thinking that all arguments are either experimental or mathematical, if he meant that the only statements admissible as premises are either mathematical equations or else facts discovered as a result of the enterprise of experimenters. Both everyday and philosophical arguments often appeal to 'what everybody knows'. Philosophers, my contemporaries would also freely admit, are exceptionally interested in the detection of ambiguities, especially in those ambiguities which give rise to philosophical confusions. So if the peculiarity of philosophical reasoning consists simply in the extent of its interest in ambiguities and its dependence upon commonplaces, then, certainly, philosophical reasoning is distinctive. But drawing attention to ambiguities and to commonplaces, they would add, scarcely counts as reasoning. It has still to be demonstrated that there are distinctively philosophical modes of reasoning, in the sense in which, say, arguing from samples or constructing a *reductio ad absurdum* are distinctively experimental and distinctively mathematical forms of reasoning.

Such a reply certainly underestimates what has already been proved. The argument to show that justifying induction by an appeal to experience must involve a *petitio*; the argument to show that a certain sentence is on one interpretation true but trivial, on another interpretation not trivial but also not obviously true—these are distinctive not merely in the sort of premises they employ, but in what they try to achieve. They issue in a conclusion which is, we might say, quasi-formal: not that a statement is false, but that it is ambiguous, meaningless, not a genuine contribution to discussion; not that an argument is fallacious, but that it is not a proof, not an explanation, not a justification. In this resides their distinctiveness.

The real controversy, however, will turn around a somewhat more puzzling group of arguments. There are certain arguments which constantly recur in philosophy—in the writings of contemporary as well as of classical philosophers—and which strike the ordinary reader as being distinctly queer, or even fishy. Philosophy is not unique in this respect; the first time we meet a *reductio ad absurdum* argument in geometry or a 'mathematical induction' we have exactly the same feeling. The structure of the argument is not apparent to us. Clearly, it is deductive, but it does not begin from a set of premises and straightforwardly derive conclusions from them—as, say, a normal argument in Euclid does. Of such arguments, as well as of analyses and reminders, Moore makes a considerable use. Consider his reasoning in 'A Defence of Common Sense'. Writing about the common sense view of the world, he argues that if we know of certain propositions that they are features of the common sense view of the world, it follows at once that they are true (*Philosophical Papers*, p. 44). This sort of argument certainly strikes one as being both queer and philosophical. To some of my contemporaries it sounds too queer to be good: thus Wisdom in *The Philosophy of G. E. Moore* (ed. P. A. Schilpp, p. 424) spoke of Moore's 'short demonstrations' as producing 'discomfort' in his readers.

Yet queer-looking forms of reasoning occupy a critical position in philosophy. If we ask why philosophers do not accept the traditional dualism of mind and body, or reject the doctrine of representative perception, or do not believe in God, we shall very often find that arguments of a queer-looking sort—for example, the infinite regress argument—play an important, and perhaps the crucial, role in their reasoning. If philosophers are often contemptuous of the philosophical productions of eminent experimental scientists; if, on the other hand, the experimental scientist with philosophical interests cannot understand why philosophers unite in rejecting conclusions which look to him so plausible, the solution often lies in the fact that there is some philosophical argument the validity of which is almost universally accepted by philosophers but which the experimental scientist cannot see as an argument at all, so unfamiliar is its structure.

Furthermore, just because they are arguments of a rather special, and sometimes extremely subtle, type, the philosopher himself can easily be misled by them. If, to take the same example, infinite regress arguments are of very great importance in philosophy, the fact remains that they are often misused; about their exact force, indeed, there can be considerable controversy. It is with arguments of this sort—deductive in character, but having certain peculiarities of structure in the eyes of experimental scientists and of untutored common sense—that I shall be particularly concerned. I hope to examine them more closely than has usually been done, to see on what suppositions they rest, how, if at all, they can be countered, and what sort of conclusions can depend upon them. I do not wish to suggest either that, in a purely formal sense, they are a peculiar species of argument, or that a philosophical position could be worked out by their use alone. But I am not prepared, either, to acquiesce in the view which Waismann put forward that 'all the proofs in a good book on philosophy could be dispensed with, without its losing a whit of its convincingness'.[1] Nor do I think that Wisdom is right to feel discomfort in their presence.

No doubt their misuse has often brought philosophy into disrepute; philosophers have tried to use philosophical arguments in cases where what is really needed is the careful experimental testing of a hypothesis or a strictly formal

[1] 'How I see Philosophy' in *Contemporary British Philosophy*, Third Series, 1956, p. 482.

analysis. That is why demarcation-issues can be important —not in order to prevent anybody from talking about anything but in order to get people to see what sort of work they will have to do if they are to make a serious contribution to a particular sort of topic. To apply philosophical reasoning-procedures is one sort of work; working with them will not help us to determine whether, say, belief in Christianity helps men to live better lives, or whether blind men can estimate shapes accurately, or whether State patronage of the arts encourages mediocrity, or whether immoral men are always unhappy, or whether tragedy purges the emotions. But it is by the philosophical sort of work, if at all, that we can hope to determine whether it is logically possible for there to be an omniscient Being, whether the theory of a representative perception is a possible explanation of our perception of objects, whether a State can have a higher existence than the people it governs, whether and in what way the judgements of critics are testable.

There can be no deductive metaphysics—let that be agreed. We cannot hope, with Spinoza, to construct a philosophy *more geometrico*. We do not now share Leibniz's belief that we shall some day be in a position, when confronted with a philosophical problem, to 'take our pencils in our hands, sit down to our slates, and say to each other "Let us calculate".' But it is quite another matter to assert that in metaphysics there can be no deductions. It would be absurd, too, wholly to overlook the contribution to philosophy of the deductive metaphysicians; for it is to them, in large part, that we owe the refinement of philosophical reasoning, and the discovery of new philosophical arguments.

Chapter Two

THE INFINITE REGRESS

MANY of the major forms of philosophical reasoning were first employed by Plato, either as a result of his reflection upon the procedures adopted by Socrates or under Eleatic inspiration. The infinite regress is no exception; we meet it in the *Parmenides*, where the following dialogue occurs:

Parmenides : I fancy the consideration which leads you to imagine the existence of these various unitary forms is to this effect: when you have judged a number of things to be large, you presumably pronounce, in a review of them all, that they present one and the same pattern, and this is why you regard the large as one thing.

Socrates : Precisely so.

Parmenides : But what of *the* large and other large things? When you pass them all mentally in review in the same fashion, must this not again give rise to the appearance of a single large something, in virtue of which they all appear large?

Socrates : Presumably.

Parmenides : Consequently a second form of magnitude will present itself, distinct alike from *just* magnitude, and from the things which participate of magnitude. On a fuller view of all these cases, we shall discover yet a further form, in virtue of which they will all be large; thus, you see, every one of your forms will no longer be one, but an indefinite plurality.[1]

I do not wish to become further involved than is necessary for my present purposes in the difficulties of Platonic exegesis; Parmenides' regress is indeed less important for me in what I take to be its actual controversial context in

[1] §132 trans. A. E. Taylor.

the *Parmenides* than as suggesting an argument which might well have been, but has not quite been, there propounded. The problem which is preoccupying Plato, very naturally in view of the intellectual situation of his time, is 'the one and the many'—the question whether, as Parmenides had argued, there is a single ultimate entity, the One, or whether, on the other hand, there is an indefinite multiplicity, as Plato takes Heraclitus to have maintained. The theory of forms can be considered, from one point of view, as an attempt to compromise in this dispute by maintaining that there is a relatively small number of ultimate entities, the forms; everything else is real only in so far as it stands in some relation—say, the relation of participation—to these forms. Then Parmenides uses the infinite regress argument in order to show that this compromise is an unstable one: that if we try to give any account of the relation between, say, the form 'largeness' and the various everyday things we call 'large', we find ourselves compelled to suppose that there is another form of largeness which is necessarily involved in the relation between the particular large objects and the original form of largeness, and hence the small group of forms turns into an infinite plurality. Thus Plato's compromise: 'a plurality, yes, but a limited plurality' breaks down.

There is, however, a more fundamental argument which is readily suggested by what Parmenides has to say, especially when it is taken in conjunction with an earlier remark in the dialogue: 'You hold, you tell me, that there are certain forms: the rest of the things around us participate in these and consequently take their denominations from them?' In the light of this remark, we can interpret the theory of forms as an analysis of predication: as a possible answer to a question which has certainly been of interest to philosophers—'how is it possible for a number of different things to have the same property in common?'—the answer, namely, 'in virtue of the fact that they are all related in a certain way to the same form'. Philosophers have very commonly supposed that there is something puzzling, mysterious, unintelligible in the fact that a number of different things can 'share the same property'; the theory of forms can be interpreted as one method of 'making predication intelligible'.

The infinite regress argument can then be used as an emphatic way of pointing out that if 'sharing the same property' is unintelligible, then so also is 'participating in the same form'. For suppose we consider any property P which x, y, z, share; and then we say that when x, y, z appear to share the property P what really happens is that they are related in a certain way to the form P. Then we have simply replaced the original property of 'being P' by a new property 'being-related-to-the-form-P'. If there is any unintelligibility attaching to the fact that x, y, z, can all share the property P, there will be exactly the same difficulty in understanding how they can all share the property of 'being-related-to-the-form-P'.[1] But this point, which could be made directly, can be developed in a forcible way—and a way which suits Parmenides admirably, since his main concern is with multiplicity—by saying that if we can understand how x, y, z, can be P only by supposing them to be related to the form P, then equally we can understand how they can all be related to the form P only by supposing them to be related to the form of 'being-related-to-P' and, then again, we can understand how they can all share the property of 'being-related-to-the-form-of-being-related to P', only by supposing them all to be related to still another form—the form of 'being-related-to-the-form-of-being-related to P'—and so on *ad infinitum*. Thus we never would be in a position to understand how x, y, z can be P. Yet this is what the theory of forms promises to make clear to us. The infinite regress argument brings home to us the fact that the intelligibility the philosopher is seeking is not to be found by going further along the path

[1] See also John Anderson: 'Universals and Occurrences', *Aust. Jnl. Phil.*, 1929, p. 138.

he has begun to tread; having failed to achieve it by introducing a single form into the situation, he is not going to do any better by introducing still more forms.

Then the point of this argument, however it be expressed, is that if the fact that a number of things can have a property in common is somehow 'unintelligible' or 'requires explanation', that unintelligibility cannot be removed by pointing to some property which they all possess, e.g. the property of imitating a form. Of course, this is so only if our problem has the generalized form characteristic of philosophy. If, for example, we are puzzled about the fact that a number of philosophers all write in a similar style, our puzzlement might certainly vanish once it is pointed out to us that they are all imitating the same philosopher. The possibility of providing an explanation of this type in empirical cases has no doubt led philosophers to suppose that if we are puzzled about the general logical problem how a number of things can share the same property then the solution to our puzzle in this case, too, lies in supposing that they have some other property in common—for example, that they are all related to the same form. But in the logical case an infinite regress is generated, as it is not in the empirical case.

If, it should be observed, a philosopher were simply to say this: 'When things have a property in common, they are always related to a form', no regress arises. It could be true, for all the regress argument can show to the contrary, that there is a form of muddiness and that all muddy things are in fact rather like this form; it could be true, even, that once upon a time somebody looked at the form of muddiness, decided that he would like there to be a lot of muddy things, and so created them—as somebody might look at a painting and then decide to make a number of copies of it. For, on these hypotheses, it is not denied that in fact the things in question are all muddy. That they came into existence in a particular way, by being copied from a model, is a historical hypothesis, no concern of logic; that

22

they are all rather like a form would be, logically speaking, an accident. The regress arises only if it is supposed that things cannot *really* have a property in common, that *really* all they can have in common is a relationship to a form. The main point of the regress argument could be set out thus: 'If things which appear to have a property in common are really all related to the same form, then since things which are really all related to the same form really have a property in common, it will follow that things which appear to have a property in common really have a property in common.' In other words, the appeal to forms, which is meant to provide a substitute for 'really having a predicate in common' quite fails to fulfil that purpose.

The argument is perfectly general. If it is valid, then it does not matter *what* property we mention, it can never be the case that the possession of this property makes it possible for things to have a property in common. If, for example, we substitute 'being called by the same name' or 'coming under the same concept' for 'being related to the same form', the force of the infinite regress is unaffected. This means that if anybody wants to have it explained to him how a number of different things can share the same property, he has to be told that this *cannot be explained*, in the sense, at least, that we cannot substitute for 'having the same property' another predicate the use of which does not already presume that things can have a predicate in common. Of course, there are other senses of the word 'explanation' in which 'having the same property' can be explained: in the sense, for example, that 'being at a philosophical Congress' can be explained by (i.e. elucidated by) 'being at a meeting where a lot of philosophers talk'. We might, that is, find another way of expressing 'having the same properties' which is, in some respects, clearer. If, for example, somebody were to say that 'having the same properties in common' means 'having qualities or relations in common' then obviously no regress is involved.

Or we might try to show, by looking more closely at the

notion of 'same', that philosophers have been *unnecessarily* puzzled by the predicate 'having the same property'. That, roughly speaking, is Wittgenstein's technique; and perhaps such a line of reasoning would have to supplement the bare assertion: 'It is impossible in principle to explain how things can have the same property in common'—a statement backed by an infinite regress argument—before that statement could be expected to satisfy the puzzled philosopher. But the importance of the infinite regress argument remains: it shows that in an important sense of 'explain' it is impossible to explain predication. If somebody says: 'I find it unintelligible that things should have the same property', there is a sense in which we have to say to him: 'that's just the way things are'. Similarly, if somebody says 'I'm puzzled why anything should exist at all', then an infinite regress argument can be used to point out that, anyhow, this is not the sort of puzzlement that can be relieved by drawing attention to the existence of something, in the way in which if someone is puzzled about there being flies in his house we might draw attention to a hole in his flyscreens.

So far, I have been simplifying, because I have been proceeding as if the infinite regress argument were entirely 'knock-down'. But of course, there are ways of evading it. For example, the following reply might be made: 'I see no difficulty in understanding how different things can have it in common that they enter into a certain relation with something. My puzzle is only about the sharing of the same quality. Hence if "x, y, z, are all P" is explained to me as meaning that "x, y, z are all related to the form of P-ness" (or all come under the concept P or are all called by the same name "P") my difficulties are completely removed. It is not necessary for me to suppose the existence of a further form to explain the possession of a common relational predicate, for this does not *need* explanation. Plato unfortunately failed to make the distinction between relational predicates and qualitative predicates but once it is made the alleged infinite regress is wholly ineffective.' Plato's argument, on this view, should read as follows: 'Things which appear to have qualities in common are really all related to the same form; things that are really related to the same form really have a relation in common. Therefore things which appear to have qualities in common really have a relation in common.'

To meet such a reply the philosophical argument has to be further developed. One might try to show, for example, that no reason can be given for extending such privileges to relational predicates; that if there is any difficulty in understanding how x, y, z, can all be P, there will be exactly the same difficulty in understanding how they can all be related to P. Or one might rather argue that any such relation will have to rest on a community of characteristics between x, y, and z; that, for example, we can account for the fact that x, y, z are all related to the form P-ness rather than to the form Q-ness only by supposing that they have qualitative peculiarities in common, which are not shared by the things related to Q-ness. I shall not now pause to consider whether these replies are adequate; but they will serve to draw attention to an important fact—that an infinite regress argument always rests on certain assumptions, in this case that relational predicates are in the same logical position as qualitative predicates.

But before looking a little more fully at the general structure of the infinite regress argument, I shall turn to examine the way it is used by certain contemporary philosophers. Consider first the following from Ryle's *The Concept of Mind*: 'The crucial objection to the intellectualist legend is this. The consideration of propositions is itself an operation the execution of which can be more or less intelligent, less or more stupid. But if, for any operation to be intelligently executed, a prior theoretical operation had first to be performed and performed intelligently, it would be a logical impossibility for anyone ever to break into the circle' (p. 30).

25

Now to Ryle's argument the following objection is sometimes raised: 'I see no reason for believing that our intelligent internal theoretical operations must in turn be preceded by another operation of intelligent theorising. Hence the alleged regress never gets going; we can stop at the point at which we have pointed out that intelligent actions must be preceded by intelligent thinking.'

This objection fails to appreciate the exact character of the position Ryle is arguing against. Against the mere assertion that: 'Every intelligent action is in fact preceded by intelligent thinking', the infinite regress argument certainly does not apply, any more than there is a regress involved in asserting that 'every happy marriage is preceded by a happy engagement'. This is simply a sociological hypothesis to be examined as such: a person can put forward this hypothesis without being at all committed to asserting that every happy engagement is preceded by a previous happy engagement. Similarly, to assert that every intelligent action is preceded by intelligent thinking is to propose a psychological hypothesis which could be criticized only by making observations and seeing whether we can discover cases where in fact intelligent actions occur without being preceded by intelligent thinking. A person who says that in fact intelligent actions always are so preceded is not at all compelled to hold that every intelligent piece of theorizing is in turn preceded by another intelligent piece of theorizing. An infinite regress argument, to put the matter generally, has no applicability to the straightforward empirical assertion that every A is preceded by a B.

But the thesis Ryle is considering is not such a straightforward psychological assertion; it is in fact what we might call a 'constitution-explanation' and these are subject to philosophical criticism. The thesis is that the intelligence of an action is somehow *constituted* by the fact that it is preceded by an intelligent mental operation: just as in the *Parmenides* case a thing's property is supposed to be constituted by its relation to a form. In consequence, we cannot possibly know that an act is intelligent without first knowing that it is preceded by an intelligent act of thinking, just as we were not able to know that a thing has a property except by knowing that it is related to a form. Then, according to the regress argument, it must equally be the case that the intelligence of the mental operation is constituted by its relation to a previous mental operation and so on *ad infinitum*. So we never are in a position to discover whether an act is or is not intelligent, although this is just what the alleged explanation set out to tell us how to do.

Now here again a certain assumption is made (parallel to the assumption that relational predicates are in the same position, in respects essential for the argument, as qualitative predicates): the assumption, namely, that what is true of the intelligence of actions is true also of the intelligence of intelligent thinking, that, for example, there is no 'privilege' attaching to the intelligence of thinking which would make it possible to 'read off' its intelligence directly. Suppose someone were to say: 'Intelligence consists in thinking syllogistically. We need only look at a piece of thinking to see whether it is syllogistic in form or not. To call an action "intelligent" is just a way of saying that it has been preceded by such a syllogistic piece of thinking.' Then the regress would not apply. Although the intelligence of actions would be constituted by their relation to preceding, intelligent, acts of mind, the intelligence of such acts of mind would not be constituted by their relation to still other acts of mind. But such a person would also really be denying that the action is intelligent in the sense in which the thinking is intelligent; Ryle has felt justified in presuming that the person who says that an action, to be intelligent, must be preceded by intelligent thinking would also say that the action is intelligent in the same sense that the thinking is intelligent. But once again we observe that an infinite regress can be evaded, temporarily at least, by claiming privilege for the first step in the alleged regress; and that to rebut this claim the philosopher has to show that there is no good reason for extending such a privilege to a particular class of cases.

It will by now be apparent that an infinite regress argument, like any other argument, has force only under relatively complex circumstances. We can, wrongly, be convinced that by it alone we can demolish a philosophical explanation when in fact we are working with an auxiliary hypothesis—the assumption that no privilege is to be claimed for any of the class of propositions to be explained —and this hypothesis our opponents will simply not admit. Thus to revert to an earlier example, they will not admit that to explain why 'anything' exists by reference to God's existence involves a regress, because, they will say, the existence of God does not require explanation in the sense in which the existence of other things requires explanation. (God is not, that is, part of 'anything'.)

The role of these claims to privilege will become a little clearer if we consider the difference between what is sometimes called a 'vicious' and a 'harmless' infinite regress: it would be better to say, an infinite regress and an infinite series. Consider such propositions as: every event has a predecessor, every event has a cause, it is always logically possible to question a proposition. Now, it is sometimes objected to assertions such as these that 'they involve an infinite regress', a regress which can only be stopped by claiming privilege for a particular event which has no predecessor (e.g. the creation of the universe) or some proposition which it is logically impossible to question (e.g. that a necessary being must exist). But in fact the regress argument simply does not apply in these cases. If to 'it is logically possible to doubt every proposition' the objection is raised: 'then it must be logically possible to doubt *this* proposition, and logically possible to doubt whether this proposition can be logically doubted, and so on'—the reply can simply be given 'and so it is'.

Similarly, if to 'every event has a cause' the objection is raised: 'But this cause will itself be a kind of event, and so must have a cause, and this event in turn will have a cause and so on', then the reply can be made: 'Yes, certainly, no regress is here involved, but only an infinite series'. What makes the difference? Why can't the 'friends of the forms' retort with equal force: 'Yes, of course, there is an infinity of forms'.

The difference is that in the case of the forms the series *has* to be a finite one, if explanation by forms is to be effective, whereas in the case of causal explanation it need not be finite. Compare the following: (1) Every event has a cause; (2) to know that an event has happened one must know how it came about. The first simply tells us that if we are interested in the cause of an event, there will always be such a cause for us to discover. But it leaves us free to start and stop at any point we choose in the search for causes; we can, if we want to, go on to look for the cause of the cause and so on *ad infinitum*, but we need not do so; if we have found a cause, we have found a cause, whatever *its* cause may be. The second assertion, however, would never allow us to assert that we know that an event has happened —although it professes to lay down the conditions under which we can make precisely that assertion. For if we cannot know that an event has taken place unless we know the event that is its cause, then equally we cannot know that the cause-event has taken place unless we know its cause, and so on *ad infinitum*. In short, if the theory is to fulfil its promise, the series must stop somewhere, and yet the theory is such that the series cannot stop anywhere—unless, that is, a claim of privilege can be sustained for a certain kind of event, e.g. the creation of the Universe. It is easy to construct similar pairs of assertions, of which one commits us to the view that some procedure *can* be carried on *ad infinitum*, the other commits us to the view that an infinite series would have to be completed before the procedure could be carried out at all. For example, (1) every term is definable; (2) one cannot understand a term unless one knows its definition; (1) every proposition has consequences; (2) to know a proposition one must know its consequences; (1) every line is infinitely divisible; (2) to move along a line we must move through all its parts. In each case, the second assertion involves a *prima facie* infinite regress, although in each case, too, the regress can, in principle, be avoided by a claim of privilege—for simple terms which are their own definition, for propositions which are their own consequence, for parts which have no parts. In each case, too, the first proposition of the pair points to an infinite series, but does not generate an infinite regress.

The difference between infinite process and infinite regress is essential, say, to Karl Popper's *Logic of Scientific Discovery*. Against the possibility of a principle of induction Popper argues as follows: 'For the principle of induction must be a universal statement in its turn. Thus if we try to regard its truth as known from experience, then the very same problems which occasioned its introduction will arise all over again. To justify it, we should have to employ inductive inferences; and to justify these we should have to assume an inductive principle of a higher order; and so on. Thus the attempt to base the principle of induction on experience breaks down, since it must lead to an infinite regress' (p. 29). This is a perfectly valid infinite regress, which can only be avoided by argument to show that the principle of induction is somehow privileged: that, as Mill suggests, it can be reliably based upon experience without needing the aid of a principle of induction, that it 'isn't a proposition at all', or something of this sort.

Now, on Popper's own view, a scientific theory is testable only if statements of a lower level of universality are deducible from it; these statements must be testable in their turn and so on *ad infinitum*. And this, he says, may look like an infinite regress. But, as he points out, no regress is involved. Of course, difficulties do arise, if we say, for example, 'we are justified in believing a proposition only if it has been tested by experience', and combine *that* with the view that 'to test a proposition by experience is to deduce from it conclusions which we are justified in believing'. For it will then follow that 'we are justified in believing a proposition only if we can deduce from it propositions we are justified in believing'; a regress applies to *this* conclusion, but not to the original assertion that 'every proposition is testable'.

As I have already suggested, it is the first step in the regress that counts, for we at once, in taking it, draw attention to the fact that the alleged explanation or justification has failed to advance matters; that if there was any difficulty in the original situation, it breaks out in exactly the same form in the alleged explanation. If this is so, the regress at once develops; whether it is so, is the point of controversy. Thus, consider Wittgenstein's argument in *Philosophical Investigations* (§239): 'How is he to know what colour he is to pick out when he hears "red"? Quite simple: he is to take the colour whose image occurs to him when he hears the word. But how is he to know which colour it is "whose image occurs to him"? Is a further criterion needed for that?' Here the original puzzle is how we know to what colour the word 'red' refers. The alleged explanation is that we find this out by having an image of 'red'. But, the argument then runs, if we need a criterion to determine to what colour the word refers, we should equally need a criterion to determine to what colour the image refers. And similarly, we might add, we should need a further criterion to determine to what colour this new criterion applies, and so on. So we could never use the criterion. To point this out *underlines* the unsatisfactory character of the original explanation and makes it perfectly clear, too, that we cannot evade the difficulty by introducing a third criterion into the story.

With these considerations in mind, we can appreciate the points raised by Waismann's recent rejection of the view that the infinite regress constitutes a philosophical proof. Waismann's essay 'How I see Philosophy' in *Contemporary British Philosophy* (Vol. 3) is of particular importance from my point of view because it is directed against the whole position that there are any 'hard arguments', as he puts it, in philosophy.

He begins by suggesting that the 'homeland' of the infinite regress argument is mathematics. As a prototype of such a mathematical argument he offers a proof that $\sqrt{2}$ is irrational:

'Let me choose as a typical case the proof that $\sqrt{2}$ is irrational. If it were a rational number, we could find two integers m and n such that

$$m^2 = 2n^2 \qquad (1)$$

We may then argue as follows. As m^2 is even, m must be even; hence $m = 2m_1$. Substitution yields

$$2m_1{}^2 = n^2 \qquad (2)$$

As n^2 is even, n must be even; hence $n = 2n_1$. Substitution yields

$$m_1{}^2 = 2n_1{}^2 \qquad (3)$$

If, then, two integers m and n exist which stand in the relation (1), they must have halves which stand in exactly the same relation (3), and these must have halves which stand in the same relation, and so on *ad infinitum*; which is plainly impossible, m and n being finite. Therefore the tentative assumption (1) cannot hold, and $\sqrt{2}$ cannot be rational. Q.E.D.' (p. 476).

It will at once be apparent that this is not at all the sort of regress we have been describing. Unfortunately, Waismann's method of presentation does not bring out the form of the argument quite clearly. As it stands, one might imagine that it is somehow inconsistent with the finiteness of a number that it should bear the same relation to a number that its half bears to that number's half. And this, of course, is not so. Twelve is twice six, six is twice three and so on *ad infinitum*; and there is nothing in this fact incompatible with the finiteness of twelve and six. The difficulty in the present case is that the halves will always have to be integers, so that m and n must be integers which have

32

an infinite number of integral halves. And this, so the argument runs, is incompatible with their being finite numbers.

This is a much stronger argument than a philosophical regress, as comes out in the fact that Waismann refers to it as being at once an infinite regress and a *reductio ad absurdum*. The more ordinary way of proving that $\sqrt{2}$ is irrational is by deducing from the hypothesis that $\sqrt{2}$ is rational that numbers exist which both have and do not have common factors. In Waismann's proof it is deduced, rather, that an integer which must exist if $\sqrt{2}$ is rational would have to be both finite and infinite. But the argument is in principle the same; some supposed entity would, if it existed, have contradictory properties, and therefore any proposition which implies that it exists must be rejected. Philosophical regresses, on the contrary, demonstrate only that a supposed way of explaining something or 'making it intelligible' in fact fails to explain, not because the explanation is self-contradictory, but only because it is, in the crucial respect, of the same form as what it explains. Or again, that a proposed criterion is of no use as a criterion, because to apply it we should need already to be able to make the kind of distinction for making which it is supposed to be necessary.

That Waismann does not appreciate this important distinction between destroying the claims of an alleged explanation and disproving the view that something exists comes out very clearly in his comments on Ryle's regress argument about acts of willing. This argument, according to Waismann, sets out 'to prove the non-existence of something', to 'do away with acts and states of mind'. But, of course, it does, and can do, nothing of the sort. Its objective is much more restricted: to overthrow the view that there *must be* acts of will if we are to explain how voluntary acts differ from involuntary acts. If, of course, there is no other reason for supposing that there are acts of will except that they are needed in this sort of explanation, Ryle's argument—if it were valid—would leave a person with *no*

33

reason for supposing that there are acts of will just as the *Parmenides* regress might leave him with *no* reason for supposing that there are forms, or might only lead him to reject *one* reason for supposing that forms exist. It does not itself disprove the existence of forms.

One might become confused on this point because in writers like Bradley the infinite regress argument is apparently used to prove that 'the world of appearances' is self-contradictory, that nothing can be Real except the Absolute. In this case, as in mathematical examples, the infinite regress argument is associated both with accusations of self-contradictoriness and with the attempt to prove something about 'Reality'. But if we look at Bradley's argument more closely, we see that in fact the infinite regress plays only a limited role in it. It would be possible to admit the validity of his infinite regresses without for a moment accepting his metaphysical conclusions. The regresses are directed, for example, against the attempt to assert that A can stand in the relation R to B only in virtue of the fact that the relation R is a third entity which unites the entity A to the entity B, when the obvious objection is that if there is any difficulty in understanding how A is related to B the same difficulty will apply to the view that A and B are both related to a third entity R. But this, of course, does nothing to show that there is a self-contradiction involved in the notion of relation, or that relations belong only to the world of appearances.

Even if every attempt to explain relations, in the sense in which Bradley is looking for an 'explanation', leads to regresses, this need not disturb us; for we may take it to mean only that relations cannot be explained—in his sense of explanation. We cannot say, without regress, that relations are possible only in virtue of the fact that they are actually qualities of one or other of the terms, or in virtue of the fact that they are entities which fall between the terms; but this is only to say that relations cannot somehow be got rid of out of the world, by being treated as a sub-species of things, or as a sub-species of qualities. Bradley himself anticipates this sort of objection: 'The arrangement of given facts into relations and qualities may be necessary in practice,' he writes, 'but it is theoretically unintelligible. . . . And it can hardly be maintained that this character calls for no understanding—that it is a unique way of being which the reality possesses, and which we have got merely to receive' (*Appearance and Reality*, p. 25). Now, of course, I am not prepared to admit either that 'the arrangement of given facts into qualities and relations' is a proper description of the situation—for to talk of an 'arrangement' is to suggest that we have been at work in the world tidily distributing it into relations and qualities—or that the 'arrangement' is a 'character of Reality'. In putting the matter in this way, Bradley is assuming his own metaphysical system. But I am asserting that there can be no question of what Bradley calls 'justifying' relations, or of 'making them intelligible', if this means showing that they are derivable from some more fundamental feature of things. Relations are not *un*intelligible, but they cannot, in the required sense, be *made* intelligible (although we can make them intelligible if all this means is helping to remove the appearance of mystery with which they are sometimes surrounded). All this is brought out in the fact that attempts to make relations intelligible, as Bradley saw, issue in infinite regresses.

To return now to Waismann. I am suggesting that he has not really seen the force, or the limitations, of the infinite regress argument in philosophy, mainly because he has wrongly identified it with a quite different argument in mathematics. But a good deal of his time, all the same, is spent in drawing attention to a point I have also emphasized—that it is, in principle, possible to evade (temporarily, at least) infinite regress arguments, especially by claiming privilege for a certain class of propositions. That is the only real ground for his final conclusion that 'no philosophical argument ends with a Q.E.D. However

35

forceful, it never forces. There is no bullying in philosophy neither with the stick of logic nor with the stick of language' (*Contemporary British Philosophy*, p. 480).

If we are prepared to say that an argument 'forces' only if there is no position one can possibly take up which will evade its conclusion, then no doubt the infinite regress argument does not force. Or rather, even that cannot be said: for if it does not force us to conclude that, say, a supposed explanation fails to explain it *does* force us to say this (presuming we accept the validity of the argument), *unless we are prepared to take a particular sort of evasive step*—to claim privileges. This connects with a wider point: that every valid argument 'forces', in the sense that it restricts freedom of movement, but that no argument forces absolutely. One can evade any empirical argument in any of a number of ways; but the argument still rules out certain possibilities, and it may in practice force us to a certain conclusion. For the means of evasion may not in fact lie open to us, even if we are well aware that they exist as logical possibilities. Pigs might fly, but we shall not wish to be drawn into asserting that they do. Similarly people can in fact be forced by infinite regress arguments to change their views, even if more ways than one of evading the argument still lie before them as logical possibilities.

Perhaps, however, Waismann's answer would be something like this: there are some arguments which can be evaded only by challenging the generally accepted rules for that type of argument—e.g. substitution rules in mathematics, or the rule that suppositions must be rejected which issue in contradictions—and only after arguments of this sort ought we to write Q.E.D. Then claiming privilege for a class of propositions is not challenging the rules, and so an argument which still leaves open the possibility of a claim of privilege ought not to have Q.E.D. written after it. But it is a long way from this to Waismann's further claim that 'all the proofs in a good book on philosophy could be dispensed with without its losing a whit of its convincingness'

(p. 482)—that the most an argument like an infinite regress can do is to point to 'a knot in thought', that 'the real strength lies in the examples'. No empirical proof, on his account of the matter, ought to have Q.E.D. written after it; it does not follow that all the empirical proofs can be left out of, say, a book on biology without its losing a whit of its convincingness.

A little later, Waismann adopts a somewhat weaker position: 'Arguments on a small scale, containing a few logical steps only, may be rigorous. The substance of my remarks is that the conception of a whole philosophical view is never a matter of logical steps' (*ibid.*). This seems to me wholly inconsistent with what Waismann has said just above—and I do not see how it is possible to maintain that a philosophy can contain rigorous arguments only if they are 'on a small scale', containing only a few logical steps. The rigour cannot somehow go out of them if they are on a larger scale or contain more logical steps.

But I do not wish to claim, in any case, that infinite regresses, or any form of philosophical reasoning, can be used to construct 'the conception of a whole philosophical view'. The role of infinite regresses is limited; sometimes they do no more than prove that a particular explanation, or a particular criterion, which somebody has proposed quite fails to accomplish what it sets out to accomplish. Sometimes, I suggest, they are more important than this: in company, anyhow, with other philosophical arguments they bring us to see the limits of explanation, what have to be accepted as 'brute facts', and the limits of criteria, what distinctions have to be accepted as just recognizable. This is always something formal: that something exists, that things have properties in common, and are related to one another, that there are continuities and discontinuities, that some propositions are true and some false. These are not conclusions deduced from an infinite regress: they are, indeed, not conclusions at all. But that they are not, and cannot be, conclusions, the infinite regress argument helps us to see.

37

Chapter Three

THE TWO-WORLDS ARGUMENT

THE GENERAL tendency of philosophy is towards monism, in one or the other of its two very different varieties. There have, of course, been distinguished dualists—Plato and Descartes, for example—but they have been the exception. Few philosophers have been satisfied with a doctrine which preserves that sort of absolute separation between the mind and the body, the eternal and the temporal, the supernatural and the natural, which is to be found in the orthodox Christian theologies. This is an important fact about philosophers; the rejection of dualism is indeed one of the few points on which almost all the creative philosophers of modern times have agreed. Why this unwonted unanimity?

I have suggested that there are two different sorts of monism; let us call them 'existence-monism' and 'entity-monism'. Entity-monism is the doctrine that 'ultimately' there is only one real entity. What we normally regard as distinct things—whether they be chairs, or musical compositions, or human beings—are, all of them, appearances of this one entity. Some philosophers describe themselves as materialistic monists, others as spiritualistic monists. But obviously this will not do. For if all differences are unreal, the one real entity cannot properly be described as material rather than as spiritual, or as spiritual rather than material. The most that can be said (if even this can be said) is that there is 'the One' or 'the Absolute'. For anybody to say: 'My monism is corporeal in type' is a contradiction in terms—if, that is, his monism is an entity-monism.

Entity-monism has had relatively few, although some distinguished, exponents. The case is quite different with

38

what, for want of a better name, I have called 'existence-monism'. Existence-monism is difficult to define in general terms. But we might put it thus: when we say that something exists, or that things of a certain kind exist, this *exist* or *exists* has an invariant meaning whatever the 'something' or the 'kind' may be, i.e. there are not sorts, or levels, or orders of existence. More accurately, what is asserted by 'X exists' can always be asserted by a proposition which contains an 'is' which has, in this sense, an invariant meaning. Existence-monism, unlike entity-monism, does admit of varieties. Philosophers might say, and have said, that to exist is to be perceived, or to be in process, or to be spatio-temporal, or to be a possible subject for physical investigation, or to be a thing with properties, and so on.

The possible variations are, one might even think, limitless; any predicate might serve. But most of them we should at once rule out. Nobody could now win credence who asserted that to be is to be a quantity of water, however plausible that doctrine might have looked to Thales. This would not be only for empirical reasons. We should not bring it against Thales' view, simply, that scientists had looked at some substance in a laboratory and found that it was not watery. The objection would run deeper: that 'to be' cannot involve the possession of some specific descriptive property (whatever qualms we might suffer if we were asked to define that phrase more exactly). Such a property as wateriness cannot have the sort of priority which Thales' theory would ascribe to it. So it is not only wateriness in particular but any similar predicate which is now being ruled out. Water is the sort of thing to which we *ascribe* existence; and 'water exists here' is not the mere tautology 'the water here is watery'.

Contrast the view that 'to be is to have a place in Space-Time'; this sort of difficulty does not arise, or not so obviously, for Space-Time is not the sort of thing to which existence is ascribed or which is used to distinguish one thing from another. 'Spatio-temporality exists here', if it means anything at all, does assert the mere identity 'this spatio-temporal region is spatio-temporal'. Of course, specific spatio-temporal predicates are used as modes of distinction—something, that is, may be distinguished from its fellows in virtue of its position, or duration, or size, or shape; but the more general property of being 'spatio-temporal' is not ordinarily a distinguishing predicate—although metaphysicians sometimes try to turn it into one by alleging that there is a non-spatio-temporal kind of existence. As for those who say that 'to be is to be an object of thought', they always pay a certain homage to the force of what I am arguing by setting out to show, in Berkeley's manner, that it would be self-contradictory to attempt to use 'object of thought' as if it were a descriptive predicate.

It is not my present object, although by now it might appear to be, to define monism and to distinguish its types. What I want to do, simply, is to consider why most creative philosophers have been attracted by some sort of existence-monism, whether it has taken the form of an explicitly argued phenomenalism, idealism, physicalism, naturalism, or has merely been the implicit assumption, certainly widespread, that the traditional dichotomies of Mind and Body, God and Nature, are obviously untenable.

The convergence on existence-monism arises, I want to suggest, because philosophers have come to accept as unanswerable a particular philosophical argument, which I have called the 'two-worlds argument', but might, more frivolously, have described as the Humpty Dumpty argument. Its basic point is that once we break up any system in a certain kind of way, it becomes quite impossible to put the pieces together again in a single situation: and yet, unless they can be so put together, the whole point of the breaking-up is lost. Such a general line of reasoning is to be found in Plato's *Parmenides* (133a–135c), in a version which, although it is somewhat obscure and unsatisfactory, has a special importance in fore-shadowing a very common type of two-world argument—a type in which the 'common situation' to which I referred is the knowledge situation.

In the theory of forms as it is described in the *Parmenides* 'existence' has a different significance according as it applies to particulars or to forms. To assert of some particular entity X that it exists is to say that some transitory event has taken place which participates in the form of 'X-ness'; to assert, on the other hand, that the form X exists is to take it to be a member of a world of eternal, unchanging and simple entities. Thus 'is there a form of mud?' cannot be answered by pointing to anything that happens, or could happen; the form has 'real being, just by itself', as Parmenides puts it, and 'no such real being exists in our world'.[1] On the other hand, the question: 'Is there mud here?' cannot be settled simply by deciding whether there is a form of mud; any answer to that question must contain a reference both to some passing occasion and to the form in which it participates. All knowledge is of forms; concerning particulars we can only have 'belief' or 'opinion'.

But now the problem arises: who can possibly be aware that a transitory event does participate in a form? For suppose there is a mind which belongs to the world of eternal objects. Let us call it 'God'. Then such a mind could never be aware that a particular participates in a form. An eternal mind can have knowledge only, not mere belief or opinion—which comes only from our imperfections—and there can be no knowledge of transitory events. God, as Aristotle later drew the conclusion, can never be aware of particulars. Yet, on the other hand, consider a mind which is part of the world of changing particulars: such a mind can never have a knowledge that is perfect knowledge. A particular mind can only imperfectly participate in knowledge, whereas it is not possible to have an imperfect knowledge of a form. As something simple, a form is either wholly known or not known at all. So nobody can ever be

[1] As translated by Cornford in *Plato and Parmenides* (1930) p. 96, 133c.

in a position to be aware that any given particular is related to any given form. Yet it is essential that someone should be aware of this, if the forms are to fill their theoretical role either as explanatory principles or as ideal standards. So the theory of forms leads to consequences which are incompatible with its *raison-d'être* as a theory.

A similar point can be made about a great many two-world theories. Thus Berkeley draws a distinction between two manners of existence: dependent existence—the sort of existence possessed by the objects of perception—and independent existence, possessed only by minds. 'Spirits and ideas', he writes, 'are things so wholly different, that when we say "they exist", "they are known", or the like, these words must not be thought to signify anything common to both natures' (*Principles of Human Knowledge*, §cxlii). Minds ('spirits') we know by 'notions', objects by 'perceptions'. But Berkeley leaves us with no way of knowing that ideas are dependent upon minds for their existence. This cannot be perceived, because that would imply that we can perceive a mind, nor can it be notionally apprehended, because that would imply that we can have a notion of an idea. Yet Berkeley has to claim to know this dependence, in order to put forward his theory at all. And if there is some third way of knowing which can comprehend both minds and ideas, there is no longer any ground for supposing that ideas and minds have to be known in different ways.

The more fundamental point against two-world theories, however, is ontological rather than epistemological. It is not only that we could not *know* any relation between the two sorts of existence, but that no such relation could occur.[1] Thus, in Berkeley's case, to assert that 'the objects we perceive are dependent upon minds for their existence' is to say that they are *in fact* thus dependent, even although men do not ordinarily perceive that this is the case. Yet

[1] See also John Anderson: 'Realism and Some of its Critics', *Aust. Jnl. Phil.*, June 1930, pp. 126–7.

that ideas are dependent upon mind is a fact about ideas, and it is only facts about minds, on Berkeley's view, that exist independently of whether they are perceived. If Berkeley is right, there can be no theory of perception, and yet his own theory is a theory of perception.

Similarly, suppose we describe the existence of particulars as here-and-now existence, and the existence of forms as eternal existence. Then take the situation: the particular participates in the form. Suppose its participation is here-and-now. Then this at once implies that the form is here-and-now. Perhaps this will be more obvious if we reverse the relationship, following the method used by Ryle in his *Parmenides* articles (*Mind*, 1939). If the particular is to participate in the form, there must also be a converse relation. Socrates in the *Parmenides* suggests that this relation is 'being present in'—the form must be present in the particular. Then the form must be here-and-now to be present in the particular, which is purely here-and-now. The form could last longer, of course, than the particular; it might move on to some other particular; but it cannot be eternal, cannot lie outside the spatio-temporal realm. As soon as the forms and the particulars are brought together in the relation of participation, they are automatically taken to belong to a single realm of being. Suppose, on the other hand, the relation is simply one of resemblance: particulars are rather like the forms. Then the two worlds split apart, and the forms became quite otiose. Everything that is needed for knowledge—things, predicates, qualities—is to be found here and now; the relation of likeness is far too loose for the purposes of the theory. Furthermore, the existence of even the loosest of relations cuts across the original two-world presupposition. For that amounts to saying that in 'Forms are . . .' this 'are' has a different meaning from the 'are' in 'Particulars are . . .'. But what then can be its meaning in 'Forms and particulars are like each other'? According to the theory there is no 'are' common to propositions about forms and propositions about particulars; yet to put the theory forward at all, it has to be presumed that there is such a common 'are'.

It is interesting to notice the way in which Cornford, in his Commentary on the *Parmenides*, tries to meet 'two-worlds' objections to the theory of forms: his gambit is one that has constantly been employed in the history of philosophy. 'Another weak point', he says, talking about the criticism that we could never know the forms, 'is the assumption that, if there is a sharp line between the two worlds, "we" are confined to the hither side of it. Our bodies certainly are, but as the *Phaedo* argued, our souls are more akin to the unseen and the intelligible. . . . Thus souls are an intermediate order of existents having a foot in both worlds and capable of knowing both' (p. 99).

Thus, when faced with the impossibility of finding a point of contact between his two realms of existence (a region in which transactions between them can take place), the philosopher invents an entity which can serve as such a region by, to use Cornford's phrase, 'having a foot in both worlds'. In the present case, the soul is said to be particular, yet eternal. The effect of setting up such an intervening entity, however, is at once to destroy the supposition that there *have to be* two worlds. As well, new problems immediately arise about the relation between the intermediate entity and both the worlds to which it is supposed to belong.

Thus, Plato had maintained that there must be unitary forms to account for the possibility of knowledge. But if there does not have to be a single eternal form of the soul, if souls can be both particular and objects of knowledge, why cannot this be true of everything else? Even if it turns out to be true, as a matter of fact, that the soul is the only example of a known particular this would be, so to speak, an accident; if, in any single instance, a particular can be known there is no general logical argument from the existence of knowledge to the existence of forms.

Secondly, not only are there many souls, but they are subject to the ordinary vicissitudes of particulars. As the *Phaedo* makes clear, they can be dragged down, corrupted, hindered, deceived: as the Eleatic stranger puts it in the *Sophist*, they can both act and be acted upon. So the soul, far from being an aid to the theory of forms, is in the end its greatest embarrassment. It destroys by its very existence the initial assumption that there is some sort of necessary connection between universality, unity, incorruptibility and eternity on the one side and between particularity, multiplicity, corruptibility and changeability on the other. In short, to suppose that there is an entity which bridges the gap between the eternal and the temporal at once destroys every argument for the existence of the gap; if the soul can belong to both worlds, there are not in the required sense two worlds at all.[1]

All the same, such 'bridge-entities', as I suggested, have constantly recurred in the history of philosophy. Consider, for example, 'spirit' in Plato's moral psychology or 'self-love' in Butler's. Suppose we say that there are two entities in the soul—an impartial reason, which is essentially contemplative, restricting itself to a consideration of the relation between universals; and passion, which can act, but cannot think, and always chooses a specific, passing, object—a 'particular'. Then it is at once clear that reason and passion cannot in any way interact with one another. Passion cannot stir reason into action because reason cannot act. In any case, passion has nothing to offer but bribes, to which reason is not susceptible. On the other hand, passion is susceptible only to bribes, so reason has nothing to say to it, no way of influencing its activities. To meet this difficulty it is supposed that there is a third entity, say self-love, which is capable of action, can be moved by

[1] In the 'theory of Reminiscence', as developed in the *Meno* (80e–82e) and *Phaedo* (72c–77d), the soul acquires its knowledge while it is a member of the 'higher world', before it is born into a body. That, presumably, is Plato's answer to the problem how we, as particulars, could compare particulars (unfavourably) with forms. But in that pre-existent stage, the soul is *still a particular*.

45

considerations of gain and loss (therein just like a passion) but is at the same time capable of thinking, of considering the general situation. But if one faculty can conjoin these powers, why now suppose that there are separate contemplative and passional faculties? Why not say that there is a single mind which sometimes contemplates, sometimes considers the general situation, and sometimes does not? Insist that nothing rational can be influenced by consideration of ends, and passion can no more influence self-love than it can influence reason; insist that what chooses ends cannot be swayed by purely rational considerations, and self-love can as little as passion be swayed by reason. In short, the introduction of a new faculty to bridge the gap only has the effect of showing that the hypothesis that there is such a gap cannot be consistently maintained.[1]

In the legal philosophy of the jurisprudentialist Kelsen, legislation acts as such a third entity. For Kelsen the law is essentially a system of 'norms', of ideals which are not, and cannot be, ingredients in our everyday world, over which they stand as rules of conduct. Yet he has at the same time to admit that laws are made, set up, by what are clearly historical, here-and-now, processes of society. For him, in consequence, 'that which takes place in the act of legislation is the great mystery of law and of the state', great mystery because without this historical process there would be no norms and yet norms are supposed to be outside history. 'One is inevitably reminded', Hagerström comments, 'of a mediaeval thinker who discusses the great mystery of the *God-man*.'[2] Hagerström's pupil, Olivecrona, sums up as follows: 'The law is a link in a chain of cause and effect. It has therefore a place among the facts of time and space. But then it cannot at the same time belong to another world. The law cannot at the same time be a fact (which it undoubtedly is) and on the other side something

---

[1] I have developed this argument more fully in my 'Reason and Inclination' (*Aust. Jnl. Phil.* 1937).

[2] *Inquiries into the Nature of Law and Morals*, trans. C. D. Broad, p. 268.

outside the chain of cause and effect'.[1] The legislative act is essential to the theory, as linking the norms with human conduct, yet the very existence of legislation breaks down that metaphysical contrast between norms and historical facts on which the whole theory depends.

The relation between natural and supernatural has presented philosophical difficulties of exactly the same sort. According to traditional theology, the supernatural is of a completely different order from the natural. At the same time, there are many transactions between the natural and the supernatural order. A natural being, commonly enough, is thought of as being able to influence a supernatural being by prayer, the supernatural as able to guide and intervene in natural processes.

Sometimes, indeed, this interaction is reduced to a single point. That is what really happens in eighteenth-century deism. As a result of the scientific work of the preceding century, there came to be a clearer conception of what was meant by 'a natural process'. Essentially, it is a process whose behaviour is describable in terms of physical laws, i.e. one which displays certain kinds of regularity, and the transactions of which with other things can be described in those same terms. Thus to allow that there can be supernatural intervention is really to deny that there are natural processes, for it means that a thing's behaviour is always subject to interventions which are not determinate. Berkeley saw this difficulty and saw, too, that it could only be overcome by denying that there are natural processes. For him, in the long run, all processes are supernatural. God does not 'intervene' in processes which normally run along without his intervention; their everyday running is a direct expression of his will.

The deists, in contrast, thought that if they could manage with *one* intervention all would be well: natural processes, they said, were created by a single divine act of will and

[1] *Law as Fact*, 1939, p. 17. See also my 'The Legal Philosophy of Hagerström' (*Philosophy*, 1961).

thereafter went their own way. Deism was widely criticized, and I should say rightly, on the ground that this one intervention was not enough for religion, which must suppose a more intimate and continuous relation between God and Nature—the kind of relation which can justify prayer, supplication, and the other processes of religion. The more fundamental philosophical point, however, is that the deist fails to grasp quite what is wrong with the traditional sundering between the natural and the supernatural. A logical impossibility is not to be condoned on the ground that it only happens once; the creation of the world is as much a transaction between natural and supernatural as is a miraculous intervention in an already created world, or the answering of a prayer. God, to create, must in some sense exist before the world is created and must then engage in a particular act; that is, God has to be described in terms of the sort of properties (involving complexity, change, temporality) which were supposed to be peculiar to the natural order. Creation is something happening, to put the matter in the most general way, and yet that they are happenings is supposed to be the distinguishing mark of the natural and the finite.

'How,' Caird asked in *The Evolution of Theology in the Greek Philosophers* (Vol. II, p. 11) 'can a spiritual being who is ever one with himself, be conceived as in any way relating himself to the divided and changeful existence of the world in space and time? How can an activity which, *ex hypothesi*, must be represented as a pure activity of thought, be at the same time a cause of motion in extended and material substances? And how, on the other hand, can such substances be supposed to react upon him or put themselves in any relation to him?' To these questions, Caird thought, there was no answer; and he concluded that the only way to save the supernatural was to find it everywhere, not in a distinct realm of existence. Paul Tillich, explaining in the second volume of his *Systematic Theology* (p. 6) why he feels it necessary to move 'beyond naturalism and supranaturalism', writes in a similar vein. Referring to various ways of interpreting the word 'God', Tillich considers first that manner of interpretation which is, he says, 'more decisive for the religious life and its symbolic expression than any theological refinement of the position.' It runs as follows: 'God brought the universe into being at a certain moment, governs it according to a plan, directs it towards an end, interferes with its ordinary processes in order to overcome resistance and to fulfil his purpose, and will bring it to consummation in a final catastrophe.' Then he goes on to explain why he rejects this kind of theology: 'The main argument against it is that it restricts the infinity of God into a finiteness which is merely an extension of the categories of finitude. This is done in respect of space by establishing a supranatural divine world alongside the natural human world; in respect of time by determining a beginning and an end of God's creativity; in respect of causality by making God a cause alongside other causes; in respect to substance by attributing individual substance to him. Against this kind of supranaturalism the arguments of naturalism are valid.'

Tillich has, I think, correctly summed the matter up. A God who can be moved by prayer might be more compassionate than anybody else but he cannot be ontologically different from other persons; and the same is true of a God that can cause, a God that can be a substance. Either there can be no interaction at all between God and man—and then God cannot play the religious role which is his sole *raison d'être*—or else he turns out to be just one finite being among others, no doubt with remarkable properties, but still a finite being, as, for example, William James concluded. Against the existence of such a being there can be no philosophical arguments. If somebody says that in outer space there is an immensely powerful, immensely wise being who intervenes in human affairs, this is simply a scientific hypothesis, like saying that there are immensely powerful cosmic rays which occasionally affect the minds and the affairs of human beings. The existence of God becomes a philosophical hypothesis—and the supposition that he exists creates philosophical problems—only when he is said to have a mode of existence quite different from that of other beings. Then the difficulty is that any transaction he can have with other entities will have to exist in a quite ordinary sense of the word in order to affect them; and this cannot be said without also treating God himself as having this same sort of finite existence.

Various forms of evasive action may be taken in order to avoid this conclusion. Some such modes of evasion are of no interest to the philosopher. If, like Kelsen in a similar case, the theologian is prepared to describe a contradiction as 'a mystery' and leave it at that, the philosopher has no more to do with him. One cannot stop a person from withdrawing from discussion, although one can demand that he does so absolutely.

A second line of defence is that these various descriptions of God's relation to the world have to be taken analogically, not literally. If God is described as compassionate this does not imply that he changes his mind about how to act, or experiences any particular sort of feeling, or suffers with us. If he is said to act this does not imply that he has desires or objectives or that anything happens to him or that he is complex or that he exists anywhere or at any time. If he is a substance, this does not imply that he has limits. He can create without being prior to, or contiguous with, what he creates, without using any material or changing himself. He can be present with us without existing here-and-now. But what then is left of these descriptions? What is 'a cause' if there is no temporal sequence, no spatial connection, no regularity (since God is not bound by law) nor any change in the agent, nor expenditure of energy? What is compassion without a change of attitude? Nothing whatever. The natural outcome of this sort of argument is a Spinozistic monism. 'For if you ask them,' wrote Spinoza, 'whether the divine will does not differ from the human will, they will reply that the former has nothing in common with the latter except in name; moreover they mostly admit that God's will, understanding, essence or nature are one and the same thing.'[1] If the difference between God's predicates and the predicates of natural objects is merely one of 'proportion', there can be no ontological gap between God and man; if it is a complete difference in kind, then the alleged 'analogues' convey nothing to us.

This, incidentally, is another important philosophical technique—what one might describe as the spelling out of analogies. It consists, fundamentally, in taking an analogy seriously and then showing that as soon as we do this the analogy turns out to be either quite uninformative or else incompatible with the theory into which it enters. Once again, this technique is exemplified in the *Parmenides* (131a–e), where Parmenides 'spells out' the analogy of participation, as an account of the relation between forms and particulars, and shows that if we take it seriously it is really incompatible with the theory of forms. Perhaps the most famous exemplification of it is in Berkeley's *Principles of Human Knowledge*: 'It is said extension is a *mode* or *accident* of Matter and that Matter is the *substratum* that supports it. Now I desire that you would explain to me what is meant by Matter's *supporting* extension. . . . It is evident *support* cannot here be taken in its usual or literal sense, as when we say that pillars support a building. In what sense, therefore, must it be taken? For my part I am not able to discover any sense at all that can be applicable to it.'[2]

There is a third mode of evasion on which I have already commented by anticipation: the attempt to set up between

[1] Epistola 54, as quoted in H. A. Wolfson, *The Philosophy of Spinoza*, Vol. I, p. 317.

[2] Pt. I, para. 16. Compare the further treatment of this analogy in the *Three Dialogues between Hylas and Philonous*, Dialogue I, in a passage which may also serve to illustrate Berkeley's use of the infinite regress argument (*Works* ed. A. C. Fraser, Vol. I, pp. 408–10).

God and world a set of intermediate creatures—'intelligences' or, as in Cudworth, 'plastic natures'. A great virtue in his own view, Berkeley thought, was that it removed the need for supposing the existence of such entities, a need which, as he saw, arose out of the attempt to explain 'how two independent substances so widely different as Spirit and Matter should mutually operate on each other.'[1] The difficulty again is that such interposers, half-supernatural, half-natural, either break down the gap they are supposed to bridge, or else they remain on one side or other of it and so fail to bridge it; they either destroy the supposition, for example, that a truly supernatural being must be eternal, or else they are no more able to enter into transactions with the natural order than is God himself.

The attempt to maintain that there are two distinct substances, mind and body, each with its own mode of existence, generates another classical case of the two-world argument, the argument against interaction. In this instance, we particularly notice the need to be very careful in our statement of the argument. In the passage quoted above, Berkeley refers to substances 'so widely different' as Spirit and Matter; but it is clear that substances which are very different in character can yet interact. It will not do to say that the mind cannot act on matter 'because the cause must be like the effect'; the lighted match, which by igniting petrol causes an explosion, is not, in any ordinary sense of 'like', like the explosion it produces.

So much is granted by G. F. Stout in his *Mind and Matter* (p. 123). 'Likeness of nature', he agrees, is not required. 'The real question,' Stout writes, 'is whether two existences can interact unless they are comprehended within a spatio-temporal whole or some such complex unity. Can there be interaction without community? To me it seems evident that there cannot.' The difficulty now is with the conception of 'system' or 'complex unity'. Why not, Ewing replies in *The Fundamental Questions of Philosophy*, say that the

[1] Dialogue III, p. 479 in Vol. I of A. C. Fraser's edition.

'mind-body' situation is itself such a system and provides all that is needed in this respect to make interaction possible?

Ryle in *The Concept of Mind* puts the two-world argument in a more fundamental way, which links it with our previous discussion. 'The problem,' he writes, 'how a person's mind and body influence one another is notoriously charged with theoretical difficulties. What the mind wills, the legs, arms and the tongue execute; what affects the ear and the eye has something to do with what the mind perceives; grimaces and smiles betray the mind's moods and bodily castigations lead, it is hoped, to moral improvement. But the actual transactions between the episodes of the private history and those of the public history remain mysterious, since by definition they can belong to neither series. They could not be reported among the happenings described in a person's autobiography of his inner life, but nor could they be reported among those described in someone else's biography of that person's overt career. They can be inspected neither by introspection nor by laboratory experiment. They are theoretical shuttlecocks which are forever being bandied from the physiologist back to the psychologist and from the psychologist back to the physiologist.' He continues thus: 'Underlying this partly metaphorical representation of the bifurcation of a person's two lives, there is a seemingly more profound and philosophical assumption. It is assumed that there are two kinds of existence or status. What exists or happens may have the status of physical existence, or it may have the status of mental existence' (pp. 12–13).

Ryle suggests in this passage that *by definition* the transaction between mind and body can belong to neither the mental nor the physical series. If the mental series is defined as containing only such transactions as are mental this is, of course, true. The two-world argument then becomes a very simple one indeed. It consists in saying: 'According to you, everything is either a part of the mental series or a part of the bodily series, and no transaction can belong to the mental series unless it is between members of the mental series, or to the bodily series unless it is between members of the bodily series. But then you have left no room whatever for transactions between the mental and the bodily series.' More commonly, however, the dualist presumes that the mental series can include any transaction in which one ingredient is mental, and the physical series any transaction in which one ingredient is physical; so that mental-physical transactions belong to *both* series. Describing my mental life I can say, 'At this moment I influenced my body' and describing my physical life I can say: 'At this moment I was influenced by my mind.' Then argument is needed to show that there is something about the conditions laid down for series-membership that would rule out this sort of double membership. But Ryle makes two points on which I have been insisting; first, that if we suppose that the mental life is known in one way and the physical in another, it will be impossible to give any account of our knowledge of the transaction between the two lives; and, secondly, that the crucial questions in the end, all the same, are not epistemological but ontological.

Mind and body are supposed to differ not only in properties, as an explosion differs from a lighted match, but in ontological status; the conditions which have to be fulfilled by a mind in order to exist, on the traditional theory, are entirely different from those which have to be fulfilled by a physical object. To assert that a physical body exists is to say that something is going on at a particular time in a particular place, something which is describable in principle by physical laws. To say that a mind exists is to say that at a particular time, but not in a particular place, something is happening which is describable only by spiritual laws, e.g. by teleological as distinct from efficient causality. Then the difficulty can be put thus: it has to be granted that in some sense the mind influences the body and vice versa. But the only force the mind has at its disposal is spiritual force, the power of rational persuasion;

and the only thing that can move it is a purpose. On the other side, a body has no force at its disposal except material force and nothing can influence it except mechanical pressure. This means that bodies cannot appeal to minds to act; they can only push; and minds cannot influence bodies by putting purposes before them, because bodies are not susceptible to this sort of influence. So there is no possible way in which one could influence the other. We cannot nominate any particular place—whether it be the pineal gland or the synapse—where mind interacts with body, because mind is no more in that place, nor next to it, than anywhere else. Yet if once we say that mind itself is spatial, subject to physical force, capable of exercising physical force, and so on, the supposed ontological contrast breaks down.

This type of argument is sometimes described as 'the argument against interactionism'. But if interactionism is simply the view that the mental can affect the non-mental —that, for example, if I am worried about something, this can affect my digestion—then it is obviously true. What the two-world argument is concerned to show is that inter-actionism cannot be true *if there is an ontological gap between the mental and the non-mental*; it is directed against the gap, not against the interaction.

Once again, evasive action may be taken. 'Psycho-physical parallelism' is the best known form of evasion. Notwithstanding appearances, the parallelist argues, there is in fact no interaction between the mental and the non-mental, for such an interaction is ontologically impossible. Mental events and non-mental events belong to two distinct series, even although the series run parallel to one another. But what does 'parallel' mean here? Not that certain events in the one series are *like* events in the other; this has been ruled out in advance. Nor that they occur in the same place, for the same reason. The only possible parallelism is a temporal one; certain events in the mental series occur at the same time as, or prior to, or subsequent to, certain events in the non-mental series. But this relation is not close enough to do justice to the admitted facts. Events in my mind are related temporally to all sorts of events, inside and outside my body; what 'parallelism' fails to explain is the *special* relation between what goes on in my brain and what goes on in my mind.

Even at the level of temporal relationships, parallelism jams into the single notion of 'being parallel' the fact that my mental operations are regularly preceded and regularly followed by such and such physical operations and the fact that they regularly occur at the same time as certain such operations. (Is my nervousness 'parallel' to the changes it produces in my stomach or to the changes in the brain which coincide with it?) But in any case parallelism does not even *look* plausible once the 'parallelism' between mental and non-mental has been spelled out into 'some temporal relationship or other'; for such a relationship holds between any two things we care to mention. Yet to make the relation more intimate—as it very clearly is—at once threatens the ontological gap.

The difficulties in the two-world thesis cannot be solved, either, by setting up a third entity in Descartes' manner—very, very subtle animal spirits. For, no matter how subtle, the problem persists of relating such spirits to mind if they are describable in terms of physical science; and if they are not, the problem of relating them to body. Or, if they exhibit the properties both of the spiritual and the physical, then again all ground has gone for supposing that the mental and the physical must belong to sharply sundered realms of existence.

It will now be apparent why so many philosophers have held some form of existence-monism, rejecting the view that universals and particulars, minds and bodies, God and Nature, belong to different orders of existence. For even to state such a theory, its exponents are obliged to destroy the ontological contrast which the theory is supposed to be setting up; and this becomes even more obvious as soon as they try to use the theory as a matter of explanation, a use which is the *raison d'être* of the theory. From this point on philosophers have said very different things: some that everything is changing and complex; others that nothing is; some that everything is describable in terms of physical laws; others that nothing is; some that existence-monism, properly understood, leads to entity-monism, others that it does not. These various paths I cannot now follow; but if philosophy can really show, by its own peculiar arguments, not by experimental inference or by mathematical deduction (and surely I have used neither of these), that dualism is untenable, it has made a contribution of the first importance, sufficient by itself to dispel the view that philosophy is either no more than personal vision or no more than analysis.

Chapter Four

SELF-REFUTATION

IT IS common enough outside philosophy to accuse some-body of contradicting himself. 'On the second page of your book,' we might say, 'you assert that Sydney is the largest city in Australia and on the fifth page that Melbourne is, and these propositions are incompatible. So you contradict yourself.' But to contradict oneself is not the same thing as to utter a self-contradictory statement. A person contra-dicts himself when he asserts *p* and *not-p* at different times and places, but he need never at any stage have put for-ward the self-contradictory proposition *p and not-p*. A person accused of asserting *p* and asserting *not-p* may some-times reply, in defence, that he has 'changed his mind'; there can be no such defence against the charge of asserting *p and not-p*. All this is cleverly brought out by Plato in the *Euthydemus* where, accused of inconsistency, Dionysodorus replies: 'And are you such a fool, Socrates, that you bring up now what I said at first—and if I had said anything last year, I suppose you would bring that up too' (287b). It takes a much stronger argument (288) to nail him down.

In mathematical reasoning, the case is rather different. There again, of course, the mathematician never asserts *p and not-p*. At most he asserts *r*, and then later discovers, or has it pointed out to him, that if *r* were true, *p* and *not-p* would both have to be true. Perhaps more com-monly, however, he is trying to prove *not-r*, and constructs his proof by showing that if *r*, then both *p* and *not-p*—to take my earlier example, that if the square root of two were a rational number, then some number would have to be both odd and even.

In both these forms, accusations of self-contradiction

play some part within philosophy. We might criticize Hume, for example, because on a certain page of the *Treatise* he says that he has no impression of the self, and on another page of the *Treatise* that he has a lively impression of the self. And we might go on to argue—otherwise indeed there will not be much point in drawing attention to the inconsistency—that Hume's theory *forces* him to say both that we have and that we do not have a lively impression of the self, so that there must be something wrong with his theory.

Similarly Aristotle argues in his *Topics* that those who hold that 'forms exist in us' are obliged to say of the forms that they both are and are not in motion, both are and are not objects of sensation (Bk. II, 113a, 27). Or in a somewhat more technical field, a philosopher might try to show, as Russell did, that a particular theory of classes must be rejected because it leads to the conclusion that some class both is, and is not, a member of itself.

In philosophy, however, allegations of self-contradiction may also take a quite different form. The philosophical critic does not always restrict himself to pointing out inconsistencies or to showing that a certain theory leads to contradictions; he frequently alleges that certain propositions—propositions, often enough, which have been put forward by his fellow philosophers—are self-contradictory *in themselves*. It is not just that the philosophers he is criticizing, at different times and perhaps through sheer carelessness, have committed themselves to contradictory propositions, nor is it simply that they have overlooked some relatively remote consequence of their position. More outrageously, they have made self-contradictory statements, as neither the mathematician nor the merely inconsistent philosopher is accused of doing.

Yet when we look at these allegedly self-contradictory utterances, we commonly find that they are not even compound propositions; they do not seem to exhibit, or to be reducible to, the self-contradictory form *p and not-p*. A classical case is the Cartesian *cogito, ergo sum*. Descartes alleges that 'I am not a thinking being' is self-contradictory. Yet on the face of it no manipulation can convert 'I am not a thinking being' into the form *p and not-p*.

Descartes's argument can be put thus: anyone who asserts that he does not exist as a thinking being is, in that very act, simultaneously asserting that he does exist as a thinking being. Descartes is not merely alleging, then, that some philosopher has asserted on one occasion that he thinks and on another occasion that he does not think, nor is he maintaining that from 'I am not a thinking being' both *p* and *not-p* follow as remote consequences, but much more than this: that to assert that 'I am not a thinking being' is somehow *tantamount to asserting* both that I am and that I am not a thinking being. Such a proposition, if this charge can be made out against it, I shall henceforth describe as 'absolutely self-refuting'. Formally, the proposition *p* is absolutely self-refuting, if to assert *p* is equivalent to asserting *both p and not-p*.

The Cartesian example, apart from its historical importance, usefully illustrates the ways in which self-refutation arguments can go astray, by relying on implicit assumptions which are by no means unquestionable—assumptions, so it will turn out, about the conditions of inquiry. Descartes calls his philosophical investigation *Meditations*; he begins by presuming that it is possible to engage upon a course of thinking. Working with this assumption, he asks himself what he can think to be the case. He can think, he argues, that his senses are all the time deceiving him, or even that he is led astray by mathematical reasoning. He regards thinkability as the test of non-self-contradiction, i.e. he interprets '*p* is not self-contradictory' as being equivalent to 'I can think *p*'. But, he then argues, he cannot think that he does not exist as a thinking being, because to think in that way he would have to *be* a thinking being. Therefore, he concludes, 'I cannot think' is a self-refuting proposition.

Now the propositions: 'I am not a thinking being' and 'I am a thinking being who thinks he is not a thinking being' are certainly contradictory. But that is not enough to establish Descartes' conclusion. What he has still to show is that anyone who asserts that he is not a thinking being must also assert that he *thinks* he is not a thinking being— or that he *doubts whether* he is a thinking being, in a sense of 'doubt' in which it is a mode of thinking.

Since he has presumed throughout his 'meditations' that he can think, no doubt it is impossible for Descartes himself seriously to contemplate, at this stage in his argument, the possibility that he is not a thinking being; that he can think has been written into the whole logic of his preceding argument—even into the very definition of self-contradiction. If he were now to say 'perhaps I cannot think' that would undermine the whole of his previous argument. Suppose, however, somebody had stopped Descartes at the first stage in his argument and challenged him thus: 'Hold on there! You say that you can think that your senses sometimes deceive you: I challenge that—I do not accept the view that you can think. You can *write down* that your senses deceive you, or *say* they deceive you, but you cannot *think* that they deceive you: indeed, you cannot think anything at all.' What could Descartes reply? If simply: 'But I must be able to think; I could not even think that I do not think unless I do think', then the answer could come again: 'But you cannot think you do not think, for you cannot in fact think."

Descartes's example is in one respect a particularly confusing one to discuss. It is fairly clear in what circumstances we are prepared to say of somebody that 'he can speak' or that 'he can write'; it is not so clear in what circumstances a person can be said to think. But let us grant that, as Descartes supposed, thinking is a specific sort of activity, quite different from talking or writing.

Then suppose somebody utters the words: 'I do not think' and is met with the objection that in order to utter such a sentence he must have thought. Obviously this objection rests on the assumption that anyone who speaks must first have thought—an assumption which would certainly be denied by anyone who denies that he thinks. Not even in the loosest possible sense of self-refutation, then, is it self-refuting to utter the words 'I do not think'.

The points at issue can be brought out by comparing the case where a person utters the words 'I do not think' with two other cases: in the first he utters the words 'I cannot speak', in the second he utters, or writes, the words 'I say I cannot speak'. In cases of the first sort the proposition 'I cannot speak' is sometimes described as 'pragmatically self-refuting'. Clearly, it is not absolutely self-refuting, on my definition. For a person who utters the words 'I cannot speak' is not asserting both that he can and that he cannot speak.

If, indeed, a person says 'I cannot speak', this is not formally different from the case when he writes down 'I cannot speak' and then the next minute begins to talk. Taking Ramsey's familiar instance, if a person says 'I cannot pronounce the word "breakfast" ' this isn't formally different from the case where he says 'I cannot pronounce b-r-e-a-k-f-a-s-t; that is very awkward when I want my breakfast at a hotel'. In both cases some action of the speaker's is the best possible counter-example to what he asserts to be the case. A person who says 'I cannot pronounce "breakfast" ' is not asserting that he both can and cannot pronounce 'breakfast'. Rather, he is asserting that he cannot pronounce it and is in the same breath pronouncing it; such same-breath counter-examples are no doubt peculiarly spectacular. But it is always logically possible for the person accused of a pragmatic self-refutation to deny that the alleged counter-example is a counter-example. 'That noise I just made,' he might reply, 'that's not pronouncing "b-r-e-a-k-f-a-s-t". That I *cannot* do.' (As a person could rightly say 'I can't pronounce "Van Gogh" '). Similarly, accused of having said 'I cannot speak', he could reply that he had a small gramophone concealed on his person; knowing he would some day lose his voice, he had spoken these words on to a record, which he now played in order to announce his dumbness. Since it is, very obviously, always an empirical question whether a person can pronounce a certain word, or whether he has uttered a certain statement, it will follow that he can always—in principle, even if sometimes with almost inconceivable hardihood—deny that he has in fact pronounced the word or uttered the statement.

Consider now the case where he writes down such sentences as 'I sometimes say that I cannot speak', 'I sometimes think that I cannot think'. Then, of course, these sentences themselves are not self-contradictory; they may well be true. But the strange thing about such remarks is that we can use them to deduce the conclusion that *what* is said, or *what* is thought, must be false.

An argument of this kind, in which a person's *admission* that he is speaking or thinking—as distinct from *the fact that* he is speaking or thinking—is used as an argument to show that what he is speaking or thinking cannot be in fact the case, we could perhaps dignify with the name of an *ad hominem* self-refutation. To 'I sometimes say that I cannot speak', we might reply 'Then you have no right to say that' or to 'I sometimes think that I cannot think', 'Then you have no right to think that', even although the statement he has actually made is certainly not, as I said, self-refuting and may even be true.

Neither a pragmatic nor an *ad hominem* self-refutation is absolutely self-refuting as I defined 'absolute self-refutation'. A person who says 'I cannot speak' is not asserting 'I can speak and I cannot speak' nor is a person who writes down 'I sometimes say that I cannot speak' asserting that he both sometimes says and never says that he cannot speak. Equally, neither 'I do not think' nor 'I sometimes think I do not think' is self-refuting. If Descartes could show that a person who says 'I do not think' is always in fact thinking, then he would have shown that 'I do not think' is pragmatically self-refuting; if he could show that a person who says that 'I do not think' is *admitting that* he sometimes thinks that he does not think then he could use this fact to prove that such a person can be compelled to admit that what he thinks cannot be true (an *ad hominem* self-refutation). Descartes has not in fact done either of these things; still less has he shown that 'I do not think' is logically equivalent to 'I think and I do not think' i.e. that it is 'absolutely' self-refuting.

Let us now turn to a second famous historical case: the accusation of self-refutation levelled against Protagoras in Plato's *Theaetetus*—against the doctrine, that is, that 'man is the measure of all things'. In that dialogue Socrates is represented as bringing forward against Theaetetus a number of self-refutation arguments which are different, although connected, in form. Consider first the following: 'For if truth is only sensation, and no man can discern another's feelings better than he, or has any superior right to determine whether his opinion is true or false but each is to himself the sole judge, and everything that he judges is true and right, why, my friend, should Protagoras be preferred to the plane of wisdom and instruction and deserve to be well-paid, and we poor ignoramuses have to go to him, if each one is the measure of his own wisdom?' (161, Jowett IV, p. 217). Socrates goes on to add that certainly in these circumstances his own procedure of dialectic would be quite absurd. His argument is an appeal to what Protagoras has a *right* to say—what I called an *ad hominem* self-refutation—but in the present case the argument is indirect. It is no longer a matter of someone admitting that 'he sometimes thinks that he cannot think' and then being forced to the conclusion that what he thinks, on his own admission, cannot in fact be the case; Protagoras has not said that 'he sometimes informs people that no one can inform anybody of anything', he has merely said that 'he *teaches* people that no one can inform anybody

64

of anything', and it has still to be shown that to teach is to inform.

Consider the following example. Somebody sets up a plate labelled 'Psychological Adviser'. We go to him, and he tells us: 'My opinion is that nobody knows anything about psychological advising.' Then we might object: 'You describe yourself as a psychological adviser; that presupposes that you know more about psychological advising than anybody else; if you now tell me that you do not, this means that you have no right to claim that you are a psychological adviser.' To which the reply could come: 'No doubt my plate will lead people to expect advice very different from the advice I actually give them. But I am performing a useful service by setting up my plate, even if it is an unusual service. I am better entitled than anybody else to call myself a "psychological adviser" because I know as much as anybody else, and what I tell people is *more useful* than what my fellow-advisers tell them. Fifty dollars, please.' He is claiming, that is, that the *prima facie* contradiction in his asserting both that he is a psychological adviser and that nobody knows more about psychological advising than anybody else is not really a contradiction.

Can Protagoras take the same way out? Can he say 'There is no inconsistency between my claiming to teach and my claiming that no one knows more than anybody else: for I can teach you in the sense of giving you better advice than anybody else, although not, of course, in the sense of acquainting you with more truths'?

This is substantially the defence of Protagoras constructed by Socrates in the *Theaetetus*. Protagoras's real position, according to Socrates, is that although things are as they appear to be, yet some appearances are better than others; if we say of some people, for example, that they are 'suffering from hallucinations', this simply means that they are having unpleasant experiences, not that they have false beliefs. A man is wiser than others, and can set

65

himself up as their teacher, if he can so change people that they replace unpleasant experiences by pleasant ones.

But, as Socrates points out, this does not really evade the original objection. For it still presumes that some men know more than others; they know more about the ways in which pleasant experiences arise. Protagoras has to say: 'If you do such-and-such you will get pleasant experiences'— he has to claim that this is in fact the case, whoever else might advise us differently. Unless, in other words, the teacher knows *something* which other people do not know— whether this be the condition under which people's experiences can be modified, or a set of truths about physical objects—he has no claim to be regarded as a teacher.

My imaginary psychological adviser can excuse himself: he can say 'I might not be able to give you psychological counsel but at least I can give you advice about psychological counselling'. Protagoras, however, has put himself in a position in which he cannot give advice about *anything*; his thesis is not the restricted empirical one that of a certain class of persons—psychological counsellors—none is wiser than any other, a thesis which can only be attacked on empirical grounds, but rather the unrestricted philosophical thesis that no one's views are more correct than anyone else's views. And certainly, if this is so, no one is in a position to tell people what is the case, whether about the best thing to do or about anything else.

There is a difference, however, between saying that 'I have something to tell you' is inconsistent with 'nobody knows more than anybody else', and saying that 'nobody knows more than anybody else' is self-refuting. Why should not we just as much conclude that 'I have something to tell you' is self-refuting? An *ad hominem* self-refutation, in other words, draws attention to an inconsistency—and the bringing out of crucial inconsistencies is an important philosophical procedure—but does not tell us which of the inconsistent propositions is true. It shows us that some person is in an impossible position but not which of his assertions to accept. To revert to the previous example, he may be wrong in believing that 'he sometimes says that he cannot speak' or that 'he sometimes thinks that he cannot think'.

Another objection raised by Socrates in the *Theaetetus* might seem to be more conclusive. It can be freely interpreted as follows: if Protagoras is right in thinking that what anyone takes to be true is true, it will follow that his opponents are right in *denying* that that which anyone takes to be true is true, since this is how matters appear to them. So if Protagoras is correct it will follow both that man is the measure of all things (since this is how it appears to Protagoras) and that man is *not* the measure of all things (since this is how it appears to his opponents). Hence his theory is in a precise sense self-contradictory.

Protagoras would undoubtedly object, at this point, that Socrates is taking for granted that notion of 'correctness' which he ought to eschew. For him, the situation should rather be expressed as follows: 'it is true for me that man is the measure of all things and it is true for other people that man is not the measure of all things', and these propositions 'p is true for x' and 'p is not true for y' are not contradictory. But the difficulty cannot be thus avoided. For even if we can make some sense of the description of p as being 'true for x'—and what can we take it to mean except that 'x thinks p is true' which at once raises the question whether it *is* true?—Protagoras is still asserting that 'p is true for x' and 'p is not true for y'; these propositions he is taking to be true. It has to be true not only for x but for everybody that 'p is true for x' since this is exactly what is involved in asserting that 'man is the measure of all things'.

The fundamental criticism of Protagoras can now be put thus: to engage in discourse at all he has to assert that something is the case. It is not just that he is pretending to have a certain social role, that of teacher or 'wise man', which he is not entitled to claim unless some people know more than others—as the psychological counsellor is pretending to a role which, on his view, nobody has. The matter cuts deeper: it is presupposed in all discourse that some propositions are true, that there is a difference between being the case and not being the case, and to deny this in discourse is already to presume the existence of the difference —since otherwise the notion of 'denying' is quite meaningless. In the present case, unlike the *Cogito* argument, this conclusion cannot be avoided by any suggestion that discourse can be carried on in some different way, by speaking or writing as distinct from thinking. As Ramsey put it: 'What you can't say, you can't say, and you can't whistle it either'—presuming, that is, that 'say' here means 'assert', and not 'speak'. The argument applies to any sort of discourse at all, as much to what Plato calls the dialogue of the soul with itself as to dialogue with other persons. We cannot in discourse renounce the claim to be able to make true statements. Only if a philosophical argument can show in this way that a sentence can propose nothing—because what it asserts, if it were taken to propose something, would be inconsistent with the presuppositions of all proposing— is it pointing, I suggest, to an absolute self-refutation. To assert that, for example, 'there are no truths' is to assert both that there are and that there are not truths because, precisely, to assert is to *assert to be true*. Similarly to suggest that 'there are no truths' is to suggest that this is true, to hint at it is to hint that it is true, and so on.

We might try to invoke against Protagoras's relativism an infinite regress argument: 'You claim it to be true for you that man is the measure of all things, but then you are saying that it is absolutely true that this is true for you, and so on *ad infinitum*.' But such a regress really presumes the point we have been directly making, that to assert a proposition is to assert that it is true. Otherwise, the reply can be ready enough: 'No, I am only saying, "It is true for me that it is true for me . . . and that this is true for me and so on".' This is substantially F. C. S. Schiller's reply to such a regress in his 'Protagoras the Humanist' (*Studies in*

Humanism, p. 314) when the regress is directed against 'the true is the useful'. The argument he is contesting is that 'the true is the useful' has to be asserted to be *true*, and his reply is that it need only to be taken to be *useful*. It is useful to believe that the true is the useful and useful to believe that this belief is useful, and so on—wherever 'true' appears in the regress it can be replaced, without difficulty, by 'useful'.

But the fact is that at every stage in such a regress something is being taken to be true: whether it be said that Schiller is an Oxford man or that it is useful to believe that it is useful to believe that Schiller is an Oxford man, at every level there is 'written in', as it were, a preliminary 'it is the case that' or a subsequent 'is true'. Either no contribution to discussion is being made at all or else something is being put forward for our consideration, something we can dispute, contradict, seek evidence for, try to prove. . . . In short it is being claimed that some proposition *p* is true. That particular claim might be rejected. We might say that *p* is false or that although we do not know whether it is true or false it is a good thing that people believe it is true—but we are still claiming that some proposition ('*p* is false' or 'believing *p* has good consequences', or 'I do not know whether not-*p* is true') is true. That claim we *cannot* renounce in discourse. We cannot simultaneously put forward propositions for discussion and assert that no proposition is true.

Similarly, we cannot renounce the claim that some of our statements are significant. Suppose somebody says, not 'You cannot understand a word I say'—which may well be true, although *if* true it will not convey anything to me—but 'no sentence conveys anything'. Then he is saying something that cannot be taken seriously, something that is not a candidate for truth, because to take it seriously would be at once to take it as being intelligible. To invite us to discuss 'no sentence conveys anything' is to ask us to consider whether *what that sentence conveys* is true. To assert that no sentence conveys anything is absolutely self-refuting: for ' "no sentence conveys anything" is true' asserts that 'what the sentence "no sentence conveys anything" conveys is true, and "no sentence conveys anything" is true.'

Sometimes it cannot immediately be seen that what professes to be a serious theory is in fact, in this sense, self-refuting; this may have to be proved by, for example, breaking down a claim for privilege. Consider Max Black's criticism in his *Language and Philosophy* (pp. 3–8) of C. I. Lewis. Lewis had argued (*Mind and World Order*, p. 75) that 'we can never really know' that other people are having the same sense experience that we are having. It may be, he argues, that I get 'the sensation you signalize by saying *red* whenever you look at what I call "green" and vice versa . . . that in the matter of immediate sense qualities my whole spectrum should be entirely the reverse of yours.' Then, Black argues, if this form of sceptical doubt has any force, it must apply just as much to phrases like 'immediate sense qualities' as to 'red' and 'green'; perhaps when you experience a sense-quality, I experience something quite different—and so on. 'And if this is so,' Black concludes, 'his view involves a very peculiar type of *reductio ad absurdum*. For if his thesis were true, it would be *meaningless* to us; therefore we cannot be expected to understand it; therefore we cannot be expected to believe it.' 'The form of this *reductio* is, of course,' he adds parenthetically, 'somewhat different from the more familiar type of argument in which some proposition is shown to entail its own falsity' (p. 7).

Black does not explain what the form of the argument is, or how it differs from an ordinary *reductio*. The peculiarity of the case, I am suggesting, resides in the fact that the argument appeals to the formal requirements of discourse. To introduce the statement p into discourse is not merely to utter sounds or write words; it is to commit oneself to 'p is a discussable utterance'. If, then, somebody tries to introduce into discourse such sentences as 'no sentences are intelligible', he cannot in fact be making a contribution to discussion; for if a sentence is to be discussable it must be intelligible. That is what is brought out by describing 'no sentences are intelligible' or 'no statements are true' as self-refuting. It is not now just a question of a pragmatic self-refutation: we don't say simply 'Look here, that very sentence you are uttering is intelligible'—for this could be questioned. Rather it is: 'that sentence, if it were true, would have to be intelligible, and so to assert it—or to suggest it as a topic for discussion—you are *forced* to maintain both that it is and is not intelligible.'

A more straightforward case, we might think, is that in which a person says: 'All universal propositions are false'. In this case, it might be said, the argument can be quite direct, proceeding not from the general conditions of discourse but from the nature of the proposition itself. For the proposition is itself a universal proposition. Hence there is a direct self-contradiction between asserting such a proposition and what is asserted in it.

In fact, however, if the argument is put in this form it is simply a pragmatic self-refutation: the form of the proposition is pointed to as a counter-example to what the proposition says. As usual, it can, in principle, be evaded by denying that the counter-example is a counter-example. Thus, invoking the theory of types, it might be replied that ' "All universal propositions are false" is not a universal proposition in the sense in which I was talking about propositions. It is a second-order proposition and it is only first-order universal propositions which I take to be false'.

The more fundamental, absolute self-refutation argument would take a quite different form; namely that 'all universal propositions are false' implies 'all propositions are false', and is hence self-refuting. Thus it might be argued, for example, that it is unintelligible to assert that 'Socrates is a man'—assuming that it is only singular propositions to which truth is allowed—unless there is some difference between being Socrates and not being Socrates, being a man and not being a man, being Socrates and being a man, and that for there to be 'differences', there must be true universal propositions, even if they are only of the form: 'Nothing which is neither A nor B nor C . . . is a man'. Some such argument, at any rate, will have to be constructed if 'all universal propositions are false' is to be condemned as 'self-refuting', in the same sense in which 'all propositions are false' is self-refuting.

Very often, absolute self-refutation arguments are directed against one form or another of scepticism. Now, of course, the word 'scepticism' is used to refer to a wide range of doctrines. People are sometimes described as 'sceptical' because they do not hold some specific belief that is current in their community, e.g. the belief in God. This sort of scepticism is not in any sense self-refuting.

At other times, a person is described as a 'sceptic' merely on the ground that he rejects some rationalistic ideal of explanation, or proof, or intelligibility. Thus when Hume is described as (or describes himself as) a sceptic this is sometimes on no better ground than that he does not believe that effects are deducible from causes. This sort of position, again, is certainly not self-refuting.

Or if somebody says 'there is no such thing as knowledge' and is met by the objection: 'But to say that is already to make a claim to knowledge', then he may well reply: 'In the sense in which I was talking about "knowledge"—the Platonic or Cartesian sense—I do not claim to *know* that there is not knowledge: I can *produce good reasons for believing* that there is not knowledge but this is not the same as claiming to know, in the Platonic-Cartesian sense, that there is not knowledge'. Or again, if he says, 'I can show you that the truth of a proposition can never be demonstrated', he can repel the objection that to show *is* to demonstrate, if he can point to non-demonstrative methods of showing.

Difficulties arise only if he says 'I can offer you a proof

that proof is impossible' and means the same by 'proof' in both cases. Then, indeed, if what he offers is a proof, it can be used as a counter-example to the conclusion that 'proof is impossible'. Here we are inclined to propose a dilemma, the dilemma which Hume calls 'that expeditious way which some take with the sceptics' (*Treatise*, Pt. IV, §1, Selby-Bigge, p. 186). 'If the sceptical reasonings be strong, say they, 'tis a proof that reason may have some force and authority; if weak, they can never be sufficient to invalidate all the conclusions of our understanding.'

Hume himself produces a characteristically 'psychological' reply to this objection. But we might restate what is substantially Hume's argument in this way: the sceptic is not obliged to claim that he can prove that proof is impossible, in a sense in which his procedure would be a counter-example to his assertion. He need only claim that he can produce an argument *as good as any other argument* to show that scepticism is true; so that if any argument were valid, his argument would be valid. The real difficulty, however, is that even this implies the validity of a certain argument, viz. the argument to show that if the anti-sceptical arguments are valid, the sceptical argument, too, must be valid. In fact, once again, the really fundamental difficulty is that an absolute scepticism is inconsistent with discourse: the argument against scepticism should point to an absolute, not merely a pragmatic, self-refutation.

To put forward a proposition is to make a statement which can be argued for and against—the argument, not the proposition, is in this sense the unit of discourse. This is connected with the fact that one cannot assert a proposition without being committed to what it implies; to say 'scepticism is true but implies nothing' is to make an unintelligible remark. A proposition is a *general commitment*; otherwise it is a mere vocable. 'Anyone who has made any statement whatever has in a certain sense made several statements', as Aristotle pointed out in his *Topics* (Bk. II, 112a, 17). But if in this sense the possibility of implication, like the possibility of truth, is already implicit in discourse, it does not at all follow that the possibility of proof, as the rationalist understands it, is so written-in. For one can certainly make an intelligible utterance without claiming either that it is self-evident, or that it follows from self-evident propositions. What is presupposed, I am suggesting, is that it is a contribution to discussion, i.e. that it can be true or false, argued for or against, contradicted or affirmed.

Is it also presupposed that we believe it? This question arises out of an argument used by G. E. Moore in his essay on 'Russell's Theory of Descriptions' (*Philosophy of Bertrand Russell*, ed. P. A. Schilpp, p. 204) about the statement 'I believe he has gone out but he has not'.[1] This, he says, 'although absurd is not self-contradictory; for it may quite well be true. But it is absurd because, by saying "he has not gone out" we *imply* that we do *not* believe he has gone out, although we neither assert this, nor does it follow from anything we do assert. That we *imply* it means only, I think, something which results from the fact that people, in general, do not make a positive assertion, unless they do not believe that the opposite is true; people in general would not assert positively "he has not gone out" if they believed he had gone out.'

Moore's argument as it stands is very strange. In the first place, Moore says that the statement 'I believe he has gone out but he has not' is both absurd and possibly true. And this is certainly a queer doctrine; in describing a statement as 'absurd' we should normally take ourselves to be excluding the possibility that it is true.

In the second place, he writes as if the question whether 'He has not gone out' implies 'I believe that he has not gone out' is to be settled by some sort of counting of heads—that if, and only if, it be true that when most people positively assert 'he has not gone out' they believe he has not gone out, does 'he has not gone out' imply 'I believe he has not gone

[1] See also C. K. Grant: 'Pragmatic Implication' (*Philosophy*, 1955).

out'. Once again it is certainly an unexpected doctrine that the question whether p implies q is to be settled by some sort of statistical investigation.

Let us consider the last point first. Now if by 'positively assert' we mean something like this: that people make an assertion in a certain tone of voice, or with a certain kind of emphasis, then one might well doubt, in these days of television commercials, political persuasion, etc. whether it is true that when people positively assert p they most often believe p. Suppose one is right to have one's doubts: let us suppose that it only occasionally happens that when people positively assert p they believe p. Does this make it all right, no longer absurd, to say that 'I believe p but p is false'? Surely not.

The fact is that to assert 'I believe he has gone out' is to make a complex claim, of which one constituent, certainly, is 'I suggest that he has gone out'. And similarly to assert in such a context as this 'but he has not gone out' is at least to say 'I suggest that he has not gone out'. I needn't *believe* this to be true but I must suggest it to be true. Now what is a person suggesting to be the case who says 'I believe he has gone out but he has not gone out'? Nothing at all. He is saying 'I suggest that he has gone out but I suggest he has not gone out'; and nothing is said here which we could possibly discuss. For this implies 'I suggest that he has both gone out and not gone out' and a self-contradictory proposition is not the sort of thing that can be suggested as a truth—indeed if a proposition is a proposal for a discussion we might rather wish to say that a self-contradictory proposition *is not a proposition at all*. There are many comparable cases, e.g. 'I remember X happening but I wasn't there', 'I promise you I'll go but I won't be there', in which the last part of the sentence really withdraws the claim made in the first part, by contradicting part of that claim. Such utterances are never made; they may all the same be constructed by philosophers to bring out, by pointing to what would not make sense, just what claim is being made by the claim

75

to believe, to remember, to promise. The essential feature about them is their unintelligibility.

Moore is quite wrong in saying they are absurd but possibly true. There are two possible ways in which 'I believe he has gone out but he has not' might be read. The first makes a stop after 'out'. We could write the utterance thus: 'I believe he has gone out. But he has not'. Then certainly these two utterances might both be true. Nor is it impossible to imagine a situation in which the two remarks are uttered successively, e.g. a situation in which we catch sight of the person concerned inside his house just as we finish uttering the first sentence. If we think of what was written above as two sentences as constituting a single statement, then that statement *could* be uttered without absurdity and could be true.

Normally, however, the 'I believe' would be taken to cover whatever follows it. Then we have 'I believe he has gone out but (I believe) he has not gone out', and this sentence is absurd and cannot be true. (Or, alternatively, if we think that a person can have two opposite beliefs, or half-beliefs, simultaneously, it is not absurd and could be true.) There does not seem to be any reading of the sentence which would make it both absurd and 'possibly true'. Assertions very like it can be true: 'Jones believes he has gone out but he has not', 'I believed he had gone out but he had not'—all these are intelligible, possible truths. They read, using the presumption I employed above, 'Jones suggests that he has gone out, but I suggest that he has not'; 'I suggested that he had gone out, but I now suggest that he had not'. But 'I believe he has gone out but he has not' simply cannot be true (and we should not call it false either) because it conflicts with a presupposition of discourse: that to be making a claim, a promise, a commitment is always to promise, claim, be committed to *some definite alternative*. It does not follow, however, that whenever I put forward a proposition for discussion this implies that I *believe* that proposition to be true—even if I usually do.

So far what we have taken to be presupposed in discourse is always something formal, e.g. that there are true propositions, that these have implications, that they convey something. The self-refuting argument, that is, has been directed only against the most thorough-going sort of scepticism. Controversial questions arise when we try to extend the range of the argument further; or more generally to consider what discourse presupposes.

The discussion of ontological commitment by philosophers like Quine turns in large part around this point.[1] For the question arises, for example, whether in any form of discourse whatever it is presupposed that there are such entities as universals, things, relations, or whether it is possible to construct languages—systems of symbols which can be used for discussing the claim that some proposition is true—which contain no symbols except proper names, or no symbols except general descriptive phrases, or no predicates except relational predicates. Sometimes arguments bearing upon this point have been closely related to issues which I raised in discussing the 'Two-Worlds' argument, in so far as philosophers have been led to suppose that what I called an existence monism implied some sort of linguistic monism, that it implies, for example, as Wittgenstein thought in the *Tractatus Logico-Philosophicus*, that discourse could be carried on in a language which contained only 'names', i.e. logically proper names, in immediate combination.

The assertion that in an ideal language every proposition consists of names in immediate combination is not, on the face of it, self-refuting; but philosophical argument bearing on it may have this much resemblance to the self-refutation class of arguments: in this case, too, what is involved is the question what discourse presupposes. It might well be argued, for example, that a combination of proper names, just because it would imply nothing, *says nothing*. Of

[1] For an example of a different sort, see the general argument of Stuart Hampshire: *Thought and Action*, 1959.

course, there can also be the more special question whether certain types of assertion, e.g. universal scientific laws, could be candidates for truth except in discourse which made certain sorts of ontological presuppositions. But in any case there is exhibited a philosophical concern with the conditions of discourse. This is one of the things which entitles one to say that philosophy has a special concern with reflection upon the work of language, and to distinguish philosophy in that way from science. But the impulse behind that concern is *metaphysical*, not linguistic.

Another important case in which there is an appeal to self-refutation is to be found in Moore's defence of common-sense. The common-sense view of the world, Moore argues, has this peculiarity: that even to say that there *is* such a view is to presume its truth—since to talk of a view as the 'common-sense view' is already to presume certain main features of that view, e.g. that there are other human beings, who share a certain belief. Thus if somebody tries to say that 'the common-sense view of the world is false' he is adopting a self-refuting position. For the use of this sentence to make an utterance presumes that there is something describable as 'a view', and this implies that there is a group of people who hold certain beliefs in common, i.e. that the common-sense view of the world is thus far true.

Moore's argument is not, however, satisfactory. For suppose we deny that anything is known to us except our own states of mind. Then we might use the phrase 'the common-sense view' to describe a state of mind we very frequently have; we might find that there are occasions when we cannot help believing that some of our states of mind, those to which we have given such names as 'other people', exist independently of us. Then by 'the common-sense view' we might simply mean the view which in these circumstances we find ourselves holding, and we might occasionally wish to remind ourselves that it is false. (Just as somebody might at intervals believe that he hears a voice speaking to him, and that it comes from a divine being: he calls his belief 'the belief that a divine being is speaking to me', but this does not imply that there is such a divine being.)

If Moore's argument were correct, it should be observed, it would equally be true that anybody who used the word 'view' at all would be committed to accepting the common-sense view of the world. To say, for example, that 'the accepted view about the earth's structure is false' would at once imply that there is 'an accepted view', and hence again that there are people who accept the view, and hence that various people exist. The only advantage in referring especially to the sentence 'the common-sense *view of the world* is false' is that this *must* be uttered by anybody who wants to reject the common-sense view whereas such a person might possibly avoid using any other sentence which contains the word 'view'.

Moore's procedure is uncomfortably reminiscent of Meinong and of certain forms of the ontological argument; we are naturally chary, now, of any attempt to deduce the truth of a proposition from the fact that a certain descriptive phrase occurs in our language. That is one reason why philosophers have so often engaged in some kind of 'analysis'—which has generally amounted to this, that they have sought to paraphrase sentences containing descriptive phrases into sentences from which those descriptive phrases are absent. For if we can say whatever we wish to assert about 'the common-sense view of the world' without actually using that descriptive phrase then it appears that nothing of any consequence can be deduced from the presence of that phrase in our ordinary way of talking. Similar considerations are involved, say, in Russell's use of the method of descriptions against Meinong.

So if we are to show that a particular position is 'incompatible with discourse', what we really have to look for are characteristics of discourse which persist through all such paraphrases, e.g. that there is a difference between truth and falsity. (This is involved even in the notion of 'paraphrasing'.) A view is absolutely self-refuting only if it is incompatible with these invariant conditions of discourse.

To sum up. Three very different types of argument have sometimes been described as self-refutations. In the first—or pragmatic—type, somebody has put forward a thesis while at the same time apparently engaging in a procedure which, according to his thesis, is impossible, e.g. he appears to speak the words 'I cannot speak'. In this instance, the person's own procedures are used as a counter-example to demonstrate the falsity of what he says. A defence is always possible: namely that the alleged counter-example is not in fact a counter-example. In the second—or *ad hominem*—type, somebody has admitted something to be the case which, if it were the case, would be inconsistent with what he says, or thinks, to be the case. It does not follow, of course, that he was right to make that admission; but he certainly has either to withdraw his admission or to grant that what he says or thinks cannot in fact be true. In the third, and most philosophically interesting case, the argument is that if we try to take some utterance seriously, we should have to regard it as at once being possibly true and as not being possibly true, e.g. to take seriously 'there are no truths' we should be obliged at once to regard this proposition as being possibly true and as not being possibly true. No evasion is possible. For to try to reply, for example, that 'there are no truths except the truth that there are no truths' would be to leave oneself open to precisely this same objection; that proposition is being put forward as possibly true, and yet it cannot be true if the only truth is that there are no truths.

Chapter Five

ARGUMENTS TO MEANINGLESSNESS: THE VERIFIABILITY ARGUMENT

IN EVERYDAY empirical arguments, or in the controversies of science, the objective, for the most part, is to show that some disputed proposition is true or false. Philosophical arguments, in contrast, frequently issue in the conclusion that a disputed proposition is neither true nor false; rather, in what turns out to be a somewhat special sense of the word, it is 'meaningless'.

Occasionally, no doubt, meaningfulness is an issue in a non-philosophical inquiry. An archaeologist, on excavating a stone which is marked with a series of scratches, might ask himself: 'Have these scratches a meaning?' and, after investigation, come to the conclusion that in fact they are meaningless, i.e. that they did not form part of any speech activity. If, however, he could translate the scratches into 'the Good is beyond all Being', this would be in his eyes sufficient proof that they are meaningful. Yet it is precisely such utterances that are condemned as meaningless by positivistically-minded philosophers.

The textual critic, too, confronted by the text of a Shakespearean play may decide that a passage in it needs to be amended, on the ground that it is unintelligible. The point can be, and often is, argued at length. Consider, for example, the Second Quarto passage in *Hamlet*:

> 'the dram of eale
> Doth all the noble substance of a doubt
> To his own scandal.'

The initial problem is whether 'eale' is a word, or a misprint for a word. For the rest, however, the passage certainly consists of words which belong to the English language; the only question is whether in this sequence they can be interpreted as making a statement. Such controversies as the following arise: whether 'scandal' can be used as a verb, whether a printer could easily mistake 'often' for 'of a', whether such-and-such an interpretation will fit into the general context of Hamlet's speech. Clearly, these are not matters on which a philosopher can be expected to have a professional opinion. Clearly, too, the textual critic would be perfectly satisfied with an interpretation which a positivist might condemn as meaningless. If, for example, the word 'substance' is employed by Shakespeare in a metaphysical sense, this fact would not give the critic pause. Yet 'substance', Hume assures us, is an 'insignificant term'. So philosophical arguments to meaninglessness cannot be assimilated to empirical arguments to meaninglessness.

There is a noteworthy passage in *An Abstract of a Treatise on Human Nature*, in which Hume most succinctly describes his own procedure: 'When he [i.e. Hume himself] suspects that any philosophical term has no idea annexed to it (as is too common) he always asks *from what impression that idea is derived?* And if no impression can be produced, he concludes that the term is altogether insignificant. 'Tis after this method he examines our idea of *substance* and *essence*, and it were to be wished that this rigorous method were more practised in all philosophical debates'.[1]

A grammarian might well be inclined to reverse Hume's argument. As evidence that philosophical terms can have a meaning without satisfying the Humean conditions, he might point to the fact that a number of the philosophical terms in our language have no clear idea annexed to them. In reply, Hume could scarcely deny that 'substance', say, is a word in our language; what he will have to reject,

[1] Ed. J. M. Keynes and P. Sraffa (Cambridge, 1938), p. 11. I have discussed Hume's positivism at greater length in Chapter IV of my *Hume's Intentions* (Cambridge, 1952).

rather, is the grammarian's identification of 'having a meaning' and 'forming part of our language'. Some words, Hume wants to say, have no right to be in the language. It is rather as if a young man were to attend classes in a University, wearing a gown, sitting for examinations, even though he has not in fact matriculated. He behaves like an undergraduate; he is listed as such; but he is not *really* an undergraduate, one might say, because he has not satisfied the conditions for entry to that class. He is a fraud, a pretender, who ought to be exposed and expelled, for all that his behaviour is so undergraduate-like. Similarly, so Hume is suggesting, although 'substance' and 'essence' behave in most respects like meaningful words, although, in particular, they take part in sentences and win a place in dictionaries, nevertheless they have not satisfied the minimal entrance requirement for being intelligible expressions.

What right has Hume, we naturally ask, to set up an entrance examination and demand a pass in it? Is he simply laying it down, quite arbitrarily, that he will refuse the title 'significant' to any philosophical term which has not a clear idea annexed to it, as some absurd old professor might refuse to admit that a woman can be an undergraduate?

Suppose, before considering that criticism, we reformulate Hume's criterion in a more plausible manner. When Hume says that a 'term' is insignificant unless it has a clear idea annexed to it, he is not using 'term' as a synonym for 'word'. Rather, in the manner of traditional logicians, he would describe as 'terms' only such expressions as can serve as the sole subject or the sole predicate in a proposition. (Of course they may have to be preceded as subjects by words like 'all', 'some', 'most', 'the'; but although such expressions grammatically form part of the subject of a sentence, the traditional logician distinguishes them from the subject as 'signs of quantity'.) So we shall not object that such vitally important philosophical words as 'if' and 'or', for all that no clear idea attaches to them, nonetheless have a meaning. The epistemological doctrine of impressions and ideas, too, is not essential to Hume's criterion; indeed, it is a distinct embarrassment to him. For it is *never* possible to point to the impression from which an idea has been derived; the impression, by its nature, has already passed away. So we might put Hume's view thus: expressions which are used as the sole subject or predicate of philosophical sentences (here, as generally in the eighteenth century, 'philosophical' includes what we should now call 'scientific') are insignificant unless we are acquainted with samples of the sort of thing which they ostensibly signify. 'Substance', for example, ostensibly signifies 'that which underlies the qualities we apprehend'; 'essence' signifies 'the inner nature of a thing'; 'causal power' signifies 'that property of the thing in virtue of which it produces its effects'. Substance, essence, causal power are all insignificant, according to Hume, because we do not experience anything which answers to these descriptions.

On the face of it, however, this way of putting the matter presumes that such descriptions have a 'sense', that they convey something to us. Hume must know what it is like to look for, and fail to find, things of these descriptions, if he is to report, as he does, that he has looked and failed to find them; failing to find a substance is not the same as failing to find a causal power, just as failing to find a unicorn is not the same as failing to find a mermaid. We cannot, by the use of Hume's method, discover whether an arbitrary collocation of letters—'zwyzyk' let us say—is significant. For we cannot look for, and fail to find, a 'zwyzyk'; we should not know where to look or when to report that we had failed to find it. Only if a word 'has an idea associated with it', i.e. only if it is used descriptively, can we possibly set about discovering whether there are things which answer to this description.

Let us make still another concession, however, by seizing upon the fact that Hume describes the word 'substance' as 'insignificant', not as 'senseless'. A descriptive expression which does not in fact apply to anything, let us now say, is

84

'insignificant'—even although it has a 'sense', in so far as it provides us with some clue as to the direction in which samples would have to be sought. When, then, Hume rejects a metaphysical expression as 'meaningless' he is drawing attention to its 'insignificance'. He is not denying that it conveys a description to us but only that the description applies to anything. Now we have come very close indeed, by our gradual amendments to Hume's thesis, to describing what actually happened in the chequered history of logical positivism.[1]

Thus Carnap tells us that when he spoke of metaphysical expressions as 'meaningless', the 'meaning' which he sought in vain was 'cognitive (designative, referential) meaning'— what we have called 'significance'.[2] He did not wish to deny that metaphysical expressions convey something to us. In the history of positivism, too, as in my re-statement of Hume, the movement has been away from talk about 'experiences' to talk about things and their properties. As well, however, the obvious objections to Hume's method, even in this revised form, have been thoroughly canvassed.

In the first place, there are objections arising from the fact that we very often wish to move beyond cases which anyone has actually encountered, either backwards or forwards in time. The biologist refers to non-filterable viruses before he can produce any samples of them; again, he develops hypotheses about the first men who lived on the surface of the earth or the first men who will land on the moon even if he cannot point to examples of such men. Expressions such as 'the first men to land on the moon'— anticipations of experience—have an important part to play in our language; to reject them as meaningless would cripple science; yet no samples answering to this description can be pointed to.

[1] Cf. Carl G. Hempel: 'The Empiricist Criterion of Meaning' first published in the *Revue Internationale de Philosophie* (1950), reprinted in *Logical Positivism*, ed. A. J. Ayer (Illinois, 1959).

[2] Note on 'The Elimination of Metaphysics', *Logical Positivism*, ed. A. J. Ayer, p. 80.

To such objections Moritz Schlick replied[1] that the impossibility of pointing to samples in such cases is only an empirical impossibility. It so happens that the scientist cannot at a particular time produce samples of viruses except by processes of filtration; it so happens that there are no fossil remains of the first men; it so happens that no one has yet landed on the moon. In the objectionable, the metaphysical, instances, on the contrary, it is not only empirically but logically impossible to point to samples. There not only *do not happen to be samples*; there *cannot be* samples, 'cannot' for logical reasons.

Now we seem to be getting nearer to the heart of the matter, to a distinctively philosophical argument. There is something very unsatisfactory about Hume's challenge when it is put in the form: 'Point out to me samples of the sort of thing which this expression ostensibly signifies.' For it might happen, only, that the person thus challenged has forgotten where to lay his hands on a sample, or that no samples are ready yet, or that he is not quite clever enough to produce one at a moment's notice. The challenge, in this form, very easily degenerates into mere assertion and counter-assertion. 'I experience no inner feeling of an underlying self', says Hume; 'I do', say his critics—and there is, at this level, no way of settling the matter. If it can be shown that it is *logically impossible* to meet with under-lying selves in our experience, the whole question is on a different footing. But how can such an impossibility be proved?

Sometimes, no doubt, the proof can easily be constructed. If, for example, 'substance' is defined as 'that which under-lies all the objects of experience', it at once follows that the metaphysician cannot point to a sample of substance. Anything to which he draws our attention would auto-matically be a particular object of experience, not some-thing which underlies such objects. Even in this case, it

[1] 'Meaning and Verification', *Philosophical Review* (1936) reprinted in H. Feigl and W. Sellars, *Readings in Philosophical Analysis* (1949).

should be observed, the insignificance of 'substance' is established by a philosophical argument—a species of 'self-refutation' argument. Anybody who says 'I can produce a sample of substance' is automatically denying that substance is the sort of thing he has taken it to be.

The logical positivists, when they spoke of 'metaphysics', had in mind an unabashed transcendentalism, the sort of metaphysics which glories in its superiority to the merely experiential, rather than the quasi-scientific metaphysics of the Aristotelian tradition. The argument to show that no sample can be produced of a transcendental object is naturally a very simple one; the logical impossibility of verification is so easily established that one may scarcely notice that it had to be established. In other cases, the whole armoury of philosophical arguments may have to be employed. Thus Carnap himself, when discussing the metaphysical use of the word 'principle', argues by 'spelling out an analogy'. He sets out to show that the attempt to point to a purely metaphysical sense of 'principle' ends by robbing the word of all its customary connotations.[1] We cannot point to samples because what was apparently an informative description turns out to be empty of content. Similarly, if 'substance' be defined not as *that which underlies all objects of experience* but as *that which gives support to the properties of things*, then, as Berkeley fully realized, it has to be shown by detailed argument that no sample of such an entity can be produced.

In general, once the verifiability principle is put in the form: 'an expression is meaningless if it is *logically impossible* to point to samples of the sort of thing which the expression ostensibly signifies', it is at once apparent that argument will be needed—and what could it be but philosophical argument?—to show that in any given case the production of samples is logically impossible. The great attractiveness of the verifiability criterion was that it seemed, by a bluff, commonsensical, 'appeal to experience', to dispense with the

[1] 'The Elimination of Metaphysics', p. 65.

87

need for the close consideration of metaphysical arguments. But it should by now be clear that this is not the case.

A further difficulty has to be met. The sample-producing criterion still seems to be too demanding. For the scientist may need to make use of such descriptions as 'the changes which will take place on the earth's surface after all human beings are dead', even although it is logically impossible to point to anything which answers to this description.[1] Hume would reply that we are entitled to refer to unexperienced entities—even to logically unexperienceable entities—if they are causally connected with what we do in fact experience. We can sensibly speak of such unexperienceable changes as are regular effects of processes now going on, or are causes of such processes. The contemporary positivist view, in its later stages, seems to be very similar; thus Hempel says that we can construe a sentence as meaningful provided only that it is logically possible to point to 'evidence' relevant to its truth. But many metaphysicians claim that they can point to things which are 'evidence for' the existence of metaphysical entities; they argue that any contingent thing will serve as evidence for the existence of a necessary being, any complex object as evidence for the existence of a Great Designer, and so on. It cannot be merely assumed that only extrapolations of a certain form—e.g. causal extrapolations—are permissible, or even that causal extrapolation can never serve as evidence for the existence of transcendental objects. Hume sees that he has to bring forward special arguments against, say, the teleological argument for the existence of God. Once again, the demand for samples is no substitute for philosophical argument; on the contrary, only by means of such arguments can it be shown that such-and-such will not suffice as a sample.

The discussion so far has turned around descriptions rather than about propositions. This may cause some surprise

[1] Cf. Russell's 'Logical Positivism' in *Logic and Knowledge*, ed. R. C. Marsh, London, 1958, pp. 373–4.

since the verifiability principle is commonly thought of as asserting that 'the meaning of a proposition lies in the method of its verification'—or at least, in the later and milder form of the principle, that 'a proposition has a meaning if and only if it is testable'—and hence as essentially a view about the meaningfulness of propositions, not of descriptions. Closer inspection shows, however, that in so far as meaningfulness is related to testability, the crucial question, always, is whether anything answers to the descriptions in the allegedly meaningless proposition (or statement, or sentence).

A sentence may be meaningless for two reasons, Carnap suggests[1]; either because it contains meaningless metaphysical expressions, or because it commits a breach of logical syntax. The second set of cases, however, does not either need, or permit of, the use of the testability argument. Take such a sentence as: 'Caesar is and', Carnap's own example. Then to say 'That must be meaningless, because it cannot be tested in experience' would be a very queer and roundabout criticism. If we cannot test it, this is only because we cannot see what it is being used to assert; that point can, and must, be made directly. The set of words does not suggest anything to us which we could set about trying, and failing, to test; 'and' does not even look like a description.

In general, allegations of syntactical meaninglessness must be based either on explicit syntactical rules—the position generally adopted in more recent logical positivist writings in which 'syntactical meaninglessness' is always 'meaninglessness *in a system*'—or else on direct intuitions, as in the Oxford appeal to what 'we cannot sensibly say'. No doubt there can be various techniques for, in Wittgenstein's phrase, 'converting concealed nonsense into *overt* nonsense'. If somebody says that 'Caesar is a prime number' is a false, but not a meaningless, assertion, then he might be met with the question: 'How could you possibly set

[1] In 'The Elimination of Metaphysics', p. 67.

about deciding whether or not *x* is a factor of Caesar?' This is about as close as one could get to a testability argument. But it really depends for its force on the presumption that 'Caesar is not divisible by *x*' is not a meaningful remark; for otherwise the impossibility of finding a way of dividing Caesar by any factor would be taken to prove that 'Caesar is a prime number' is false, not that it is meaningless. In any case the alleged meaninglessness of the original sentence could equally well be brought out by other methods; by, in Carnap's own manner, substituting the definition of prime number for 'prime number' and then pointing to the meaninglessness of the resulting sentence, or by drawing some such consequence as: 'Then when Caesar died, a prime number died' and rejecting that as meaningless, or in a number of other ways. So there is clearly no special connection between syntactical meaninglessness and the logical impossibility of testing.

Questions of verifiability, in fact, arise only if a sentence is syntactically admissible, i.e. only if it is a *prima facie* statement. But then if samples can be pointed to which answer to the descriptions the *prima facie* statement contains as subject and predicate, the statement must be testable. Suppose it has the form: 'Anything which is X is Y', then it can be tested if we can construct the argument 'Anything which is X is Y, this is an X, and so is a Y', and the only thing which can stop us from constructing such an argument is that there are in fact no true propositions of the form 'this is an X'. So if a *prima facie* statement is untestable, this must be because it contains descriptions to which, as they are used in that statement, nothing answers. To prove that a *prima facie* statement is untestable, we have to show that nothing can answer to the descriptions it contains.

Let us now reconsider the question how this can be proved. There are three distinct cases. In the extreme instance, the expression in question is actually self-contradictory; and no doubt the weirder sort of metaphysician will occasionally make use of expressions of this sort—'that which is both intelligible and not intelligible'. In the second class of cases, the description, on investigation, turns out to be empty of content. The meanings of its constituent words are so refined away by metaphysical re-definition that there is no longer any possible way of discovering whether anything answers to the description: it no longer directs us anywhere in particular. In the third class of cases, there is an incompatibility between the nature of the description and the possibility of its applying to any particular instance, e.g. there can be no true propositions of the form 'this is a transcendental being' because a transcendental being is so defined that it can never appear as a 'this', something to which attention can be drawn, a sample, a particular case. Or in a weaker, epistemological, form the criticism runs that we could never be in the position to assert 'this is a transcendental being' as something we knew to be true because that would imply that we could have direct experience of a transcendental object.

Now that we have put the matter thus, it will be very apparent that, as I have been arguing, philosophical argument is usually necessary in order to establish that for logical reasons nothing can answer to a certain description. In the extreme instance, indeed—that in which the metaphysical description is explicitly self-contradictory—no argument is needed; but, more commonly, it will have to be shown that the descriptions are equivalent to self-contradictory expressions, or that they are empty of content (by 'spelling out analogies'), or that they cannot be exemplified in particular cases (by two-world arguments). One should not merely assume, for example, that a 'religious experience' cannot be an encounter with a transcendental being. In general, then, the philosophical problem is to show that some *prima facie* description cannot in fact apply to anything—and this the verifiability principle cannot of itself demonstrate.

Suppose, however, the point can be established; certain metaphysical expressions, let it be presumed, can be proved not to apply to anything. What follows from this? To revert to our earlier question about Hume, will it then be merely arbitrary to assert that such expressions, or *prima facie* statements which contain them as subjects or predicates, are meaningless?

The general tendency in recent discussions has been to emphasize the element of arbitrariness in the verifiability principle. Even earlier, Popper put forward his 'principle of refutability' as a method of demarcation, not as a method of dismissal.[1] Propositions form *no part of science*, he argues, unless it is logically possible to refute them; but it would be quite arbitrary, according to Popper, to conclude that they are therefore meaningless. A proposition can be suggestive, even true, and yet unscientific because irrefutable; many of the assertions made by Marx and Freud, as well as more obviously metaphysical assertions, are, he thinks, of this suggestive-irrefutable kind. Similarly Ayer has said of verification arguments that 'the most that has been proved is that metaphysical statements do not fall into the same category as the laws of logic, or as scientific hypotheses, or as historical narratives, or judgements of perception, or any other commonsense descriptions of the "natural" world. Surely it does not follow that they are neither true nor false, still less that they are nonsensical'.[2] McIntyre, writing from a very different point of view, considers that it is a definite advantage to theology that such sentences as 'Providence governs the world' can no longer, after positivist criticism, be compared with scientific hypotheses.[3]

[1] See his 'Philosophy of Science: A Personal Report' in *British Philosophy in the Mid-Century* ed. C. A. Mace (1957).

[2] Editor's Introduction to *Logical Positivism* (1959), pp. 15-16. This is a long way from the confident dismissal of metaphysics as nonsense in *Language, Truth, and Logic* (1936).

[3] In his essay on 'The Logical Status of Religious Belief' in S. Toulmin *et al.*, *Metaphysical Beliefs* (Oxford, 1957). See also *New Essays in Philosophical Theology* ed. A. Flew and A. McIntyre (Oxford, 1955). I have commented on that latter volume, in ways relevant to what I am now suggesting, in my 'Christianity and Positivism' (*Aust. Jnl. Phil.* 1957) and on Karl Popper's view in 'Karl Popper's Logic of Scientific Inquiry' (*Philosophy*, Oct., 1960).

It would certainly be ironical—a 'contradiction of history' if ever there was one—if the verifiability principle should turn out to be the sturdiest method of defending that absolute distinction between the realm of science and the realm of religion which so many theologians have earnestly sought to establish and against which positivism was originally in large part directed. Are we now to say that there are religious propositions, metaphysical propositions, scientific propositions and that religious propositions are subject to criticism only by theologians, metaphysical propositions by metaphysicians, scientific propositions by scientists? So that assertions which are scientifically meaningless can none the less be metaphysically or theologically meaningful?

One point must be admitted at the outset. No philosophical reasoning can show that an expression is meaningless. For since it is a matter of convention, only, how an expression is used, it is always logically possible that a new use will be found for an expression—a new use which satisfies any criterion of meaningfulness we care to lay down. Thus, for example, a person might continue to use the phrase 'providential escape' long after he has ceased to believe that there is anything answering to the theological definition of 'Providence', or he might remark that 'Providence moves in mysterious ways' when some incompetent person, as a result of a series of unexpected accidents, is rocketed into prominence. When Hume says that 'substance is insignificant' he does not want us to stop writing such sentences as 'The substance of the matter is. . . .' A hesitating young man might be thus encouraged : 'After all, only the Absolute is perfect. Jane will make as good a wife as you're likely to get'.

Secondly, or so I previously suggested, even to argue that it is logically impossible to produce anything of the sort to which an expression refers, one has to treat the expression as a description and, so far, as having a sense. On further reflection, indeed, one might feel inclined to retract that statement. For although the expression 'that which is both intelligible and not intelligible' is made up of phrases which can serve to describe—'intelligible' and 'not intelligible'—and although the syntactical form 'that which is both X and Y' is perfectly in order, one might well want to deny that the whole expression has a sense, that it is a description. Or similarly, if Berkeley can show that 'underlying' in the phrase 'underlying experience' conveys nothing, or, more generally, if a critic can show of any *prima facie* metaphysical description that it has been refined beyond the possibility of application, then we might well conclude that 'it has no sense' or 'is not really a description at all'. At first, we might say, we thought that these phrases had a sense—because we interpreted them in a commonsensical way—but philosophical argument issues in the conclusion that they have, in fact, no sense at all. But even then we are left with a class of metaphysical expressions which it would seem to be arbitrary to dismiss as senseless, with cases where we have to set about showing that nothing could answer to a reasonably definite metaphysical description.

'Would seem to be arbitrary,' I said, but the fact is that 'arbitrary' itself is not exactly defined. 'If someone were to draw a sharp boundary,' writes Wittgenstein, in his *Philosophical Investigations*, 'I could not acknowledge it as the one that I too always wanted to draw, or had drawn in my mind. For I did not want to draw one at all. His concept can thus be said to be not the same as mine, but akin to it. The kinship is that of two pictures, one of which consists of colour patches with vague contours, and the other of patches similarly shaped and distributed, but with clear contours. The kinship is just as undeniable as the difference' (§ 76).

This is always the story when somebody offers us an 'exact definition'; it is not so much, though, that we did not want to draw a distinction as that we did not *need* to do so. The need arises only if we set out to think systematically—as we seldom do. If somebody sets out, for example, to examine systematically the different forms of human activity, including sporting activities, and in the course of so doing defines a 'game' as a 'competitive activity involving the risk of losing and the chance of winning', then this would have the consequence that neither patience nor ring-a-roses would be 'games', although we have been accustomed to describe them as such. Would this be an example of arbitrariness? Suppose the definer dealt with us thus: he brought out the analogies between bridge, football and billiards; he helped us. to see how unlike bridge and patience are, how like are patience and 'playing a poker-machine'; or that ring-a-roses is not at all like football but very like folk-dancing. Then might not we say: 'I see what you are driving at; patience is something I play but it isn't a game; ring-a-roses is a form of group amusement but isn't a game'. Might not we come to feel, in that way, that his definition is not at all arbitrary?

Similarly, I should say, Hume and the positivists, when they said that expressions are meaningless if they do not refer to anything we encounter in experience, were pushing us along a path we were already inclined to take. Reading Hume's criticism of 'causal power', we might easily say to ourselves: 'then that's really a quite meaningless conception, referring to nothing at all'. Philosophers had already said as much about 'substantial form' and 'occult quality'. Hume does not have to use much force; the phrase 'meaningless jargon' is not unfamiliar to us. It is not *wholly* arbitrary to assert that sentences which contain 'insignificant' expressions are meaningless, or that a *prima facie* description which cannot apply to anything has no sense.

Yet, on the whole, the famous distinction of propositions into true, false and meaningless, often regarded—if quite unhistorically—as one of the great glories of twentieth-century philosophy, has been a misfortune. For one thing, these three predicates are not of the same order; true and false are alternative descriptions of statements, of sentences, that is, which are *already known to have a meaning*. For another thing, it is so apparent that the sentences of metaphysicians are not 'meaningless' in certain very familiar senses of that word—the words they contain are part of a language, the grammar is impeccable, the sentences are connected with their context—that the real force of the positivist case has often been obscured.

Suppose, for such reasons, we no longer try to use the verifiability principle as a major premise in arguments to meaninglessness. What then, if at all, does it help us to see? Only this, on the face of it: that there are many metaphysical statements which cannot be discussed in the manner characteristic of science, because so to discuss them, to try to test them, would involve pointing to samples of the kinds of things which the descriptions in the metaphysical statements ostensibly signify, and this is logically impossible. Even then, I suggested, a simple application of the verifiability argument does not suffice to establish this conclusion. For it has first to be shown that it is *in fact* logically impossible to produce appropriate samples; that, for example, the workings of the eye cannot serve as a sample of the creative work of a divine being, or that mystical phenomena cannot be samples of 'communions with the Absolute', or that particular objects cannot be samples of 'participants in a Form'. The verifiability principle rather points to a question which has to be answered ('How can samples be produced which answer to such-and-such a description?') than provides us with a principle we can use to show that this question cannot, in a given case, be answered satisfactorily.

Let us take it, then, that the verifiability principle lays down a condition which has to be satisfied by expressions which play a certain part in science, and that it does not do this quite arbitrarily but in a way that pays some respect to our ordinary feeling for what is and is not a science. Does it then, after all, simply act as a way of drawing a line of demarcation between the scientific and non-scientific, as Ayer now supposes? More than this, I think. For what verifiability arguments emphasize is that certain expressions, familiar though they may be in our language, cannot, when they are ostensibly used in a certain way, serve as the key expressions in sentences which are used to describe, explain, or predict. Or one might rather put it thus: there is an inconsistency between supposing that such expressions can be interpreted in a certain way, and supposing that they can be used in a certain way.

That this is what is really involved comes out in Carnap's discussion of the word 'God'.[1] In its *mythological* use, he says, 'God' has a clear meaning. It refers to physical beings who inhabit certain parts of the earth's surface, but have rather special powers; whether there are such beings, and whether it is they and not something else which produces certain effects, can therefore be empirically tested. In its *metaphysical* use, on the other hand, although 'God' is explicitly defined, there is no way of determining whether anything satisfies the definition. Therefore, we might add, nobody is ever in a position to say 'God is at work here'; to assert anything of God implies nothing, explains nothing, predicts nothing and therefore does not describe. For to say, for example, that an event is 'the work of God' only if it favours the virtuous, or only if it is bound to lead to good results, or only if it is the work of a being with such-and-such characteristics, is at once inconsistent with the supposition that God is the Unconditioned, the Omnipotent, and so on. In *theological* sentences, Carnap suggests, there is a certain oscillation; God is sometimes treated as if he had the characteristics of the gods of mythology—as if he could be placated, influenced, made angry—and sometimes as if he were a metaphysical Being. This, we might go on to argue, is no accident; for the mythological being is the only possible object of religious practice, and yet, if he is mythologically conceived, everyday empirical arguments (e.g. those based on the predominance in the world of evil) are sufficient to show that this mythological being

[1] 'The Elimination of Metaphysics' in Ayer, op. cit., p. 66.

cannot have the characteristics which would make him a *worthy* object of religious practices.

So the positivist arguments, if backed by other forms of philosophical reasoning, do not merely show that religious truths are not scientific hypotheses, a conclusion which, as McIntyre says, the theologian ought really to welcome. They do more than that: they show that religious statements cannot be used as theologians have commonly wanted to use them—as at once giving us some sort of information about a transcendental Being and serving as a basis for explaining, predicting, describing, justifying forms of human activity. The very consideration that makes them untestable—the fact that it is logically impossible ever to say of a transcendental Being that he is here rather than there and so to refer to a situation as 'this' in which he is particularly present—makes them unusable in explaining, predicting, describing and justifying. That still leaves open the possibility that religious expressions will continue to be used; perhaps out of habit, as merely conventional phrases; perhaps as a vivid way of conveying, let us say, the uncertainties of the human situation; perhaps because people find, as Braithwaite has suggested, that to call up the images associated with these expressions helps them in moments of difficult moral choice. But it also leaves open the possibility that religious expressions will fall into complete disuse, as expressions like 'substantial form' and 'occult quality' have fallen into disuse.

To sum up. Hume and the positivists after him have failed to produce any general argument to show that certain expressions are meaningless. Indeed, this cannot be done, because it is always possible to give an expression a new meaning. Nor does their argument *by itself* even succeed in showing that, when used as equivalent to a certain specific description ('in a certain sense'), some expressions have no meaning. For to say of an expression that it is, or is equivalent to, a certain description is already, in any ordinary sense of the word, to assert that it is 'meaningful'. But the positivist arguments draw our attention to the fact that the expressions used by metaphysicians sometimes have this peculiarity: that it is logically impossible to point to samples of anything which answers to the description conveyed by those expressions. Even this much a verifiability argument cannot by itself establish; other forms of philosophical reasoning are needed in order to show that it is logically impossible to produce samples which answer to the description in question. Coming to see by such conjoint arguments that no such samples can be pointed to, we see at the same time that the expressions cannot serve as the key points in sentences which are used to explain, predict, describe, or justify. Realizing this, we may either find an alternative use for the expressions or drop them entirely from our language. No philosophical argument, by itself, can force us to take one of these steps rather than the other.

Chapter Six

ARGUMENTS TO MEANINGLESSNESS:
EXCLUDED OPPOSITES AND PARADIGM CASES

AT THE beginning of the *Monadology*, Leibniz argues as follows: 'There must be simple substances, since there are compounds; for a compound is nothing but a collection or aggregate of simple things'. As it stands, Leibniz' argument has an arbitrary air. On the face of it, every compound could be a compound of complex things; thus there could be compounds even if there were not simples.

Suppose, however, Leibniz' argument were recast in a 'formal' or 'linguistic' mode. It might run as follows: 'Our language contains the adjective "complex"; "complex" can act as an adjective—i.e. can distinguish one thing from another—only if what is complex can be contrasted with what is not-complex, the simple. Thus, from the fact that the word "complex" plays a certain role in our language, it follows that there are simples.'

Pretty obviously, this would be a bad argument, for the reasons advanced by Wittgenstein in his *Philosophical Investigations* (§47). Our ordinary way of using the word 'simple' and 'complex' is such that we contrast a simple problem with a complex problem; a simple character with a complex character; a simple design with a complex design—and so have plenty of occasions for contrasting the 'simple' and the 'complex'. But the problem, the character, the design, is neither 'simple' nor 'complex' in some metaphysically absolute sense of the word. Indeed, 'simple' and 'complex' are not contradictory descriptions; a plastic tumbler can be simple in design and yet complex in molecular structure. Metaphysicians have wanted to say that there are some entities—the 'objects' of Wittgenstein's *Tractatus*, the 'simple natures' of Descartes' *Regulae*, the 'elements' of Plato's *Theaetetus*—which are simple in a sense which prevents them from also being complex. 'But what,' Wittgenstein asks, 'are the simple constituent parts of a chair?—The bits of wood of which it is made? Or the molecules, or the atoms?—"Simple" means: not composite. And here the point is: in what sense "composite"? It makes no sense at all to speak absolutely of "the simple parts of a chair".' And again: 'Asking "Is this object composite?" *outside* a particular language-game is like what a boy once did, who had to say whether the verbs in certain sentences were in the active or passive voice, and who racked his brains over the question whether the verb "to sleep" meant something active or passive.'

Wittgenstein will not allow, I take it, that metaphysics is itself a 'language-game'. It would be as improper, on his account of the matter, for the metaphysician to assert that 'everything is complex' as for him to assert that 'some entities are simple'. Yet on the face of it, the metaphysician can produce *arguments* against the view that 'some entities are simple', e.g. the sort of argument which Plato brings forward in the *Sophist* and the *Parmenides*, and we can, at least, understand what these arguments are about. 'Simple' and 'complex' play a part in the metaphysician's 'language-game' which is rather different from the part they play in our everyday talk about designs, or characters, or problems —or chairs and tables—but it does not follow that the metaphysician's remarks are senseless. Yet one can see why Wittgenstein should think that they are. Take the metaphysician who says: 'Everything is complex'. 'Complex' cannot be, in this sentence, a distinguishing adjective—as it is in 'a complex design'. The metaphysician is, indeed, ruling out the possibility of using 'complex' to distinguish one sort of thing from another thing. Yet this is precisely how we ordinarily do use adjectives in general, and 'complex' in particular. In telling us not to use 'complex' in a distinguishing way the metaphysician, it might be suggested, is telling us to do what cannot be done—'cannot' because it cuts across 'the grammar of "complex"'.

Aristotle was aware of this particular problem. In his *Topics*, discussing the ways in which a definition can be criticized, he writes: 'Next, for destructive purposes, see whether he has rendered in the property any such term as is a universal attribute. For one which does not distinguish the subject from other things is useless, and it is the business of the language of "properties", as also of the language of definitions, to distinguish' (Bk. V, §2, 130b). Yet even in this passage Aristotle still refers to 'universal attributes', as if not every attribute had to distinguish.

Frege, on the other hand, raises a formal objection to the conception of 'universal attributes'. 'It is only in virtue of the possibility of something not being wise,' he writes in *The Foundations of Arithmetic*, 'that it makes sense to say "Solon is wise". The content of a concept diminishes as its extension increases; if its extension becomes all-embracing, its content must vanish altogether. It is not easy to imagine how language could have come to invent a word for a property which could not be the slightest use for modifying the description of any object at all' (trans. J. L. Austin, p. 40e).

A good deal depends on what Frege means in this passage by 'the possibility of something not being wise'. Two interpretations suggest themselves. On the first, there must *actually* be something that is not wise, if the description of Solon as 'wise' is to make sense; on the second, all that is necessary is that something's not being wise should be *conceivable*. If, as seems most likely, the first is the correct interpretation—that 'not-wise' must have an actual extension if 'wise' is to be intelligible—an obvious difficulty at once arises. What of such predicates as 'possessing an extension which is not all-embracing'? Are we to say that assertions such as 'this concept has not an all-embracing extension' have no sense, since nothing has an all-embracing extension? If so, Frege's own argument would be unintelligible.

Admittedly, this predicate consists of a complex phrase, not a word. But that seems to be an accident. Aristotle, supposing that some predicates have, and others have not, an all-embracing extension, might well have invented words to refer to the two distinct cases, or his translator might have done so. Let us suppose that the translator used the word 'properties' to mean 'predicates which have not an all-embracing extension' and the word 'transcendentals' to mean 'predicates which have an all-embracing extension'. Then a Frege arises, who wishes to deny that there are any predicates which have an all-embracing extension. It will be natural for him to say: 'All predicates are properties', or 'There are no transcendentals'. But then, it would seem, it immediately follows that what he is saying must be unintelligible, since if he is right there is nothing to which the predicate 'being a transcendental predicate' applies, and so the description 'being a predicate-property' has no use. But it would clearly be an extraordinary doctrine that once some philosopher had divided things in a certain kind of way, it was impossible for anybody else— on pain of unintelligibility—to reject the view that they could be divided in that way.

Let us look then at the second alternative: suppose Frege is arguing that it must be 'conceivable', as distinct from being actually the case, that something should not have a certain predicate, if the use of that predicate is to be significant. Here, of course, the word 'conceivable' is by no means clear. But it is reasonable to presume, at least, that whatever anyone has ever conceived is conceivable; so that if philosophers have maintained, and have got others to believe, that there are simple entities, then it is conceivable that there are 'simple entities'; if they have suggested, and won agreement to the view, that some concepts have an all-embracing extension, then it is conceivable that some concepts have an all-embracing extension. Then to demand only that a predicate should have a 'conceivable' opposite will not rule out metaphysical assertions and counter-assertions about the complexity of all things as 'senseless'—as Wittgenstein wanted to do.

Wittgenstein, all the same, was drawing attention to an important fact: the metaphysician is not using the word 'simple' as we use it in our non-metaphysical thinking. By itself, that settles nothing, but at least it emphasizes the peculiarity of the metaphysical use, which might otherwise escape our notice. It drives us to consider how the metaphysician does use 'simple' and 'complex', which involves, of course, a close consideration of the actual arguments by which metaphysicians have sought to establish, or to overthrow, the supposition that there are simple entities. Such an examination soon makes it apparent that when metaphysicians have described ideas, natures or forms as simple, they have taken the consequence to follow that we cannot be mistaken about those ideas, natures or forms. This is not surprising, for in the everyday use of the word 'simple', a 'simple' design is one we can easily describe, a 'simple' character is one we can easily understand, a 'simple' problem is one we can easily solve—in each case, then, the reference is to something about which we are unlikely to make mistakes. But the *metaphysically* simple is that about which it is logically impossible, as distinct from merely unusual, to be mistaken. Why should this be? Because in knowing the metaphysically simple entity at all, we know it completely; and this in turn is because all true descriptions of it are synonymous, i.e. we cannot, as we can in the case of complexes, know that it is of a certain description while overlooking the fact that it is also of some other description.

It turns out, then, that 'simple' is a predicate of a distinctly peculiar kind; to say that 'this entity is simple' is not to say that it possesses the descriptive property of being simple. If there were such a property, it would at once follow that no entity could possess it, since any entity which did would be describable as being 'simple' as well as being the sort of entity it is—say, a red sense-datum—and so would not be simple; it could be described in either of two non-synonymous ways, as 'red' or as 'simple'. To call an entity 'simple'—in the metaphysical sense—is not to describe it but to make a logical point about it, the point that only one empirical description can be offered of it.

If we wish to say, against the doctrine of 'simples', that 'every entity is complex', then too, we are not, in the ordinary fashion, offering a description of things: we are making the logical point that every entity can be described in a variety of ways. Asked to list the properties of animals, we should not include in our list 'they are complex' (any more than we should include 'they have properties'); asked to define an animal, we could not use 'complex' as our genus. If 'complex' appeared in a definition, it would serve, like 'thing', as a linguistic filler—'an organism is a complex which . . .'—not as the descriptive part of the definition. Aristotle was right, then, to point out that 'it is the business of the language of properties, as also of the language of definitions, to distinguish'; but he was also right not to conclude that there are no 'universal attributes'.

For, we are suggesting, there is a wide class of propositions—metaphysical propositions—where the use of a predicate does not presuppose that there is something to which the predicate does not apply. 'Everything is describable' does not imply that there are indescribables; this proposition is not senseless, either; and there is a point in uttering it, in so far as there are metaphysicians who have taken the view that some entities are indescribable. 'Everything that happens is natural' does not imply that there are things which are not natural—or things which have the property of not-happening—but rather that any happening is describable in terms of physical laws and spatio-temporal occurrences. But the predicates, in these cases, turn out to be of an unusual, formal, kind. Their 'content' is that propositions of a certain form are true, not that some thing is distinguishable from some other thing in virtue of possessing a special property—a characteristic which could be used in classifying or defining it.

But are such metaphysical propositions the only ones in which there are universal predicates? To say that such predicates as 'possessing a mass' or 'being in motion' are also universal predicates would at once arouse protests; for it is very commonly supposed that there are entities such as 'thoughts' and that to those entities the predicates of physics have no application. But let us suppose that they did have a universal application. Would it then be senseless to apply them at all? It would seem not. For in distinguishing between the mass and the velocity of objects we do not in any way rely upon the fact (if it is a fact) that there are some objects which lack mass or velocity. In this case, too, the predicate 'possessing a mass' would be of no use to us in classifications and definitions—or more generally, in those processes of discrimination and identification which are normally our major concern; but it need not even be pointless to remark 'that thing has a mass'— for somebody might wrongly have supposed that it was an exception—and certainly it could be a scientifically interesting statement that everything has a mass. The doctrine that a predicate cannot be both useful and have an all-embracing extension seems to rest, indeed, upon the supposition that predicates can only be used to discriminate and to identify classes of objects.

With these general considerations in the back of our mind, let us look at certain recent attempts to use the 'excluded opposites' argument as a rapid way of ruling out, as senseless, a diversity of philosophical positions.[1] Thus, writing about 'The Objectivity of History' in *Mind* (1955) Christopher Blake maintains that it is logically impossible to take the view that no historical writings are objective,

[1] See also C. K. Grant: 'Polar Concepts and Metaphysical Arguments' (*Proc. Ar. Soc.*, 1956).

since it would make no sense to talk about 'non-objective' history unless there is 'objective' history. Blake is going a lot further than Frege. Frege said only that *something* must be not wise if the assertion 'Solon is wise' is to have sense; Blake is arguing that *some historical writings* must be objective if the phrase 'non-objective history' is to have any sense.

What Blake could properly have said, and this is sufficiently obvious, is that if all history is non-objective, then 'non-objective' cannot serve as a differentiating predicate within history. Phrases like 'Macaulay's non-objective *History of England*' will then be of no use in discriminating between Macaulay's historical writings and the historical writings of, say, Ranke. But it could still be useful to describe all historical writings as 'non-objective', in order to distinguish them from the writings of physicists. There may be some point, even, in using the phrase 'Macaulay's non-objective *History of England*', although it will not be a classifying or defining point.

Suppose, for example, it is true that 'All men are fallible' or that 'All accountants love accuracy'. The consequences will follow that 'fallible' is of no use for distinguishing between men, or 'accuracy-loving' for distinguishing between accountants. But the statement 'We fallible men ought always to check quotations' or 'Accuracy-loving accountants naturally dislike vague financial estimates' are in no way logically-improper. 'Fallible' and 'accuracy-loving' have in these statements a reminding function, not a discriminating function; but it is perfectly proper to use predicates as a way of reminding.

If, then, when Ryle writes in *Dilemmas* (p. 95) that 'ice could not be thin if ice could not be thick' he means that it would be senseless, or logically-improper, to describe ice as 'being thin' unless some ice is thick, he is clearly mistaken. (Compare 'Ice could not be cold, if ice could not be hot'). Quinine is always bitter; silk is always soft; men are always mortal—yet one can say 'He drank down the bitter quinine as if it were lemonade'; 'the soft silk was soothing to the touch'; 'we mortal men do act absurdly, in that we care for the future'. If all ice were thin, then certainly we should not put up a notice: 'The ice is thin', but we should still have to remind children or imprudent adults: 'Beware, ice is thin!'

In a certain range of cases, however—including some philosophically important cases—the existence of an opposite seems to be 'written into' the sense of a predicate. The most obvious instances are predicates like 'counterfeit', 'imitation', 'copied'. Thus, to take Ryle's example, there cannot be counterfeit money unless there is legal money. 'All Icelandic coins are counterfeit' cannot be true because it would be equivalent to 'All Icelandic coins are imitations of Icelandic coins'. Even then, it is worth noting, if 'All Icelandic coins are counterfeit' simply means that 'All the Icelandic coins circulating *at the moment* are counterfeit', this could be true. Suppose the coinage is entirely silver-metallic; in principle, a gang of forgers could completely replace it by a nickel-metallic coinage, melting down the silver. But they must have something to copy, i.e. there must at some time have been genuine Icelandic coinage. Similarly, even although the original manuscript of Shakespeare's plays does not survive, it makes sense to speak of what we do in fact have as 'copies' only on the presumption that there was such an original. The argument in this instance, however, is not from the general logical principle that every predicate must have an 'opposite' but from the special characteristics of a particular class of predicates.

An unusually explicit presentation of 'the argument from excluded opposites' or 'the principle of non-vacuous contrasts' is to be found in Malcolm's essay on 'Moore and Ordinary Language'.[1] The argument, as he presents it, refers only to certain kinds of predicate. 'Certain words of our language,' he says, 'operate in pairs, e.g. "large" and

[1] *The Philosophy of G. E. Moore* (ed. P. A. Schilpp, pp. 345–68).

"small", "animate" and "inanimate", "vague" and "clear", "certain" and "probable". In their use in ordinary language, a member of a pair *requires* its opposite—for animate is *contrasted* with inanimate, probability with certainty, vagueness with clearness' (p. 364). Suppose, then, a philosopher tries to persuade us that 'all statements are vague'; he is really proposing, according to Malcolm, that we give up our ordinary use of the predicate 'vague'—for that is, precisely, to *distinguish* within the class of statements between those which are vague and those which are not. There would be nothing to gain from accepting the philosopher's proposal, he objects, for if we did we should have to invent another pair of distinguishing words to take the place of 'clear' and 'vague'—so as to be able still to distinguish, say, between statements like 'Shakespeare was born at Stratford-on-Avon' and statements like 'Shakespeare's genius lies outside space and time'.

Malcolm's is, on the face of it, a quite moderate and reasonable objection to what is certainly, if he is right, a very strange philosophical procedure. If it be true, as Malcolm argues, that 'when the philosopher says that words are really vague, he is proposing that we never apply the word "clear" any more, i.e. proposing that we abolish its use', we might well complain that we cannot easily get along without it. But in fact, of course, one does not find that a philosopher who says that 'all statements are vague' no longer praises certain utterances for their clarity or condemns the vagueness of others. Similarly, even if a philosopher denies that any empirical proposition can be certain, this does not prevent him from saying, for example: 'One thing's certain: Jones won't get a scholarship'. Is this merely because not even the philosopher himself can take his linguistic innovations seriously?

A contrast, and a comparison, with the practice of scientists now suggests itself. Scientists quite often drop *both* of a pair of contrasting opposites, replacing them—for scientific purposes—by a reference to a difference of degree on a sliding scale. Thus they replace 'hot' and 'cold' by 'degrees of temperature', 'loud' and 'soft' by 'number of decibels', 'fast' and 'slow' by 'feet per second' and so on. But, of course, the scientist does not give up using the contrast-words in all circumstances. If he is talking informally about his work he might well say: 'the lab. gets pretty hot with all that stuff cooking, and noisy, too; I'm out of it fast enough when five o'clock comes, I can tell you.' Nor does the scientist commit himself to such utterances as 'everything is really hot', 'everything is really fast', 'everything is really loud' when he discovers that the familiar contrast-predicates of everyday life are unsatisfactory in serious scientific descriptions. Nor is a motorist, even if he gives up talking about 'steep hills' and 'slight hills' as distinct from 'hills of such-and-such a gradient', tempted into the assertion that 'Really, all hills are steep'. Simply, the ordinary distinction does not discriminate enough for the motorist's purposes and is too indecisive in its application to a range of cases. Everybody would agree that a hill with a grade of one in five is 'steep', but when it comes to a grade of one in twelve, a cyclist, a pedestrian, a lorry-driver, the owner of a small car, a racing driver are likely to describe it in very different terms.

A similar situation can arise in regard to the pairs of opposites in which philosophers are interested. Thus in *The Brown Book* (p. 87) Wittgenstein writes: 'Looking at it as we did just now, the distinction between automatic and non-automatic appears no longer so clear and final as it did at first. We don't mean that the distinction loses its practical value in particular cases, e.g. if asked under particular circumstances: "Did you take this bolt from the shelf automatically, or did you think about it?" we may be justified in saying that we did not act automatically and give as an explanation that we had looked at the material carefully, had tried to recall the memory-image of the pattern and had uttered to ourselves doubts and decisions. This may *in the particular case* be taken to distinguish automatic from non-automatic.' So a distinction which we might at first have supposed to be one we could readily make in regard to any action at all turns out, if Wittgenstein is right, to be applicable only in a certain range of cases. But how absurd it would be to conclude that all action is really automatic—or, for the matter of that, really non-automatic—when the truth of the matter, only, is that the distinction between automatic and non-automatic is not in every case a useful one.

Something, we begin to feel, has gone wrong. Philosophers cannot be as foolish as they are now being made to appear; it cannot really be the case that they are exhorting the ordinary man to drop such words as 'clear' from his vocabulary, or trying to persuade him no longer to distinguish between cases where he picks up a book automatically and cases where he picks it up because it looks interesting. Such assertions as 'all statements are vague' *cannot* mean what, as ordinary men and women, we should naturally suppose them to mean; the counter-examples are so obvious, and so often and so explicitly drawn to our attention, that it is impossible to suppose that even the loftiest of transcendentalists could overlook them.

In fact, of course, we have been forgetting that philosophers are addressing themselves to the community of their fellow-philosophers, not to humanity at large. It is as if an economist were to be rebuked for overlooking the fact that a person can 'demand' something which he has no means of paying for. If 'all statements are vague' is in some respects queer, this is because it is a response to a—less apparent—queerness, or to a very special definition of clarity.

When Ramsey said that although we can make many things clearer, we cannot make anything clear, he was, considered from the standpoint of ordinary language, very obviously mistaken. There are a great many occasions on which we could rightly claim that we have made something clear to somebody; yet in the context of philosophical controversy, Ramsey's remark was called-for, sensible and true. We cannot 'make anything clear' if that means formulating it in such a way that it is logically impossible for anybody to misunderstand us, and that is the sort of 'clarity' Ramsey's philosophical contemporaries were looking for. 'All statements are vague' is a perfectly natural response to the attempt to construct statements which are 'clear' in this very special, philosophical, sense of the word. One could no doubt formulate the same point in a somewhat different way, by saying something like this: 'On the criterion of "clarity" you suggest, no statement could ever truly be described as "clear".' But to dismiss 'all statements are vague' as senseless, by an appeal to the principle of excluded opposites, would be quite to ignore the contribution of that statement to philosophical controversy.

In a similar way, the statement 'No bodies are solid' is, considering the history of the idea of solidity, a quite natural way of making the point that there are no bodies which are wholly impenetrable. 'No empirical propositions are certain', similarly, is an emphatic way of asserting that it is always logically possible for an empirical statement to be false. Only by considering how such statements are actually used in philosophical controversy can we possibly hope to understand them; we need to know the history behind them. But they are none the worse for that. The crucial point is that they are not attempts to purge the language of everyday life—to rid it of words like 'solid' and 'certain' and 'clear'; rather, they are emphatic ways of pointing out that particular philosophical criteria of solidity, certainty, clarity are never in fact satisfied. Nor do they make that point in an outrageous, wilfully paradoxical way; on the contrary, they make it in the most natural manner, if the historical context of controversy is taken into account.

To sum up: there is no general argument from a predicate's having no opposite to its being 'senseless', or even useless. If a predicate has no opposite, then it will, indeed, be useless *for certain purposes*—as a mode of distinguishing between or of identifying particular kinds of thing. That fact is worth pointing out; but it does not follow that such a predicate is useless for all purposes. Predicates may be used to remind, or to make a formal point, or to reject a *conceivable* classification, as well as to distinguish and identify. Philosophers have their special concerns, and in devoting themselves to these concerns they, in particular, may need to use non-distinguishing predicates or to deny that a predicate, if used in a certain way, will in fact distinguish. But in this latter case, they are not denying that the predicate can also be used in a differentiating way, although their mode of expression may easily lead, if the controversial context is ignored, to the supposition that they are doing so.

Very similar considerations apply to the 'paradigm case' argument. This argument, too, is stated in a particularly clear way by Malcolm in "Moore and Ordinary Language". He distinguishes between two classes of expression: those which could be learnt through descriptions and those which must be learnt by reference to cases. 'It is probable that' and 'It is certain that' belong, he argues, to this second class; we can learn how to use these expressions only by being shown cases where they apply and cases where they do not apply and seeing the difference between them. So it is then senseless for a philosopher suddenly to assert 'No empirical statements are certain'. We know when to use 'certain' of empirical statements; we have learnt to do so from being shown cases. There cannot possibly be no such cases; for then we could never have learnt how to use the word 'certain'.

Then are we to conclude that there must be 'ghosts' since, again, people know how to use that word correctly? The correct use of 'ghosts', Malcolm would reply, could be learnt by description; we could simply be told 'if you were to see a being with such-and-such characteristics, you would be seeing a ghost'. A person can intelligibly deny that it is possible to see a ghost; he can argue that those who profess to have done so were really suffering from an illusion. In contrast, a philosopher cannot sensibly deny, as some have tried to do, that it is possible to see a cat; he cannot sensibly suppose that everybody who has ever thought he has seen a cat was the victim of a strange sort of hallucination. 'When he says that a man does not *really* see a cat', writes Malcolm, 'he commits a great absurdity; for he implies that a person can use an expression to describe a certain state of affairs, which is the expression ordinarily used to describe just such a state of affairs, and yet be using incorrect language' (p. 358).

Malcolm has presumed, however, that there is a sharp distinction between what is learnt ostensively and what is learnt descriptively. In fact, the two sorts of learning ordinarily go hand in hand. Consider the situation of a child brought up in a society in which it is firmly believed that miracles are of daily occurrence. Then he will certainly learn how to apply the word 'miracles' by reference to cases: someone has a narrow escape from an accident, or recovers unexpectedly from an illness, or a house is saved, by a sudden shift of wind, from being burnt to the ground, and the child will be told 'that's a miracle'. But at the same time he will learn that miracles involve supernatural intervention.

Similarly, a person could learn the use of the phrase 'possessed by the devil' in a purely ostensive fashion. When he sees somebody behaving in a strange fashion he is told: 'that man is possessed by the devil'. Hippocrates, presumably, learnt how to use the phrase 'the sacred disease', by watching epileptics. So when Hippocrates wanted to say 'there is no sacred disease', the paradigm-case exponents of his day would certainly reply: 'When a man says that there are no sacred diseases, he is committing a very great absurdity, for he implies that a person can use an expression to describe a certain state of affairs, which is the expression ordinarily used to describe such a state of affairs and yet be using incorrect language'.

But, Malcolm might reply, even if Hippocrates did in fact learn to use the phrase 'the sacred disease' ostensively, he *could* have learnt it descriptively. The fundamental question, then, is whether there are in fact any expressions which could only be learnt ostensively, so that we could never have learnt them unless there are cases to which they apply. That question, in its full extent, we need not discuss; it will be sufficient to suggest that the philosophically-interesting phrases to which Malcolm explicitly refers are certainly not so ostensively tied. The phrases 'material things', 'it is possible that', 'it is certain that' could certainly be learnt descriptively. 'Material things', indeed, plays no part in ordinary language. It is a philosopher's phrase; Berkeley was so far right when he argues that in denying material things he was not denying anything which the ordinary man believes. Our parents say to us: 'Bring me a chair', 'Bring me my book', but never 'Bring me a material thing'. Unless they are philosophers, we shall never hear the phrase from their lips, except, perhaps, in referring to the tastes of the philistine—'He cares only for material things'—and that phrase, certainly, could be explained to us descriptively. When we first hear of 'material things', in any other sense, it is as things which, for example, are 'solid and extended', i.e. we meet the phrase as a philosophical description.

As for 'it is certain that' and 'it is probable that' these phrases are learnt both in cases and through descriptions. If we misuse them, we are corrected in either of two ways. Suppose we say: 'It is certain that Jones will write a great poem', then we might be told, simply, that this is not the sort of thing anybody can be certain about. Or the rebuke may be generalized. 'It is wrong to say that anything is certain if there is the slightest possibility that it will not happen', i.e. there is an appeal to an explicit criterion.

In that way a clash may arise between cases and criteria. The same thing happens with miracles, or sacred diseases, or diabolic possessions. On the one side, no one would wish to deny that men are sometimes, quite unexpectedly, not killed in accidents, nor that houses which look as if they cannot possibly escape a fire may none the less do so; nor again that people sometimes suffer from epilepsy; nor that they become insane. No one wishes to deny, that is, that there are circumstances which it is, or was, conventional to describe by the expressions 'miracle', 'sacred disease', 'diabolic possession', and that we might have been taught to use these expressions precisely by reference to such cases. What we may well wish to deny, however, is that these cases satisfy a certain criterion: that the house or the man was saved by divine intervention, that the disease is a gift from the gods, that there is a demon inside the person who is 'possessed by a devil'. We know the circumstances in which it is conventional to use the expressions; we are not denying that there are such circumstances. But we wish to deny that in these circumstances a particular supernatural agency is at work. Or on the practical side, we may wish to deny that prayer, reverence and exorcism are the best ways—as they were the conventionally appropriate ways—of dealing with difficult situations, epileptics and madmen. Yet the criteria and the methods of handling have been taught along with the circumstances of correct employment. So it is perfectly natural for us to say: 'There are no miracles, no disease is sacred, nobody is ever possessed by a devil' rather than that 'miracles do not involve divine intervention, sufferers from the sacred diseases are not stricken by the gods, people possessed by the devil have not a supernatural being inside them.'

Similarly, a philosopher may on reflection decide that the criterion of certainty he has been taught when he was told 'It is wrong to say that anything is certain if there is the slightest possibility it will not happen' has in fact no application. Or that whereas he has commonly supposed that 'seeing a cat' involved some sort of direct confrontation with the cat's qualities, no such direct confrontation ever occurs. Then it is not merely arbitrary for him to express his conclusions—whether they are correct is not our present concern—in the form 'No empirical propositions are certain'; 'No one ever really sees a cat'.

It is true that the philosopher has a choice. He *could* say, instead, 'Some of the ordinary criteria for certainty, or the ordinary criteria for seeing, will have to be abandoned'—he could, that is, go on using the expressions 'empirically certain', 'seeing a cat' but without accepting what are ordinarily regarded as implications of 'I am certain that . . .' or 'I see a cat'. To some extent, that has happened with 'miraculous' and 'possessed'; we say of a narrow escape that it is 'miraculous', or of a man who works with ferocious energy that he is 'a man possessed'— just as we allow that a man can be 'inspired' without supposing that there are Muses. As I said in discussing 'providential', no philosophical argument can lead to the conclusion that an expression must be banished from the language. But neither can it issue in the conclusion that an expression *must* be retained. Newton was able to assert that no bodies are free from gravitational influences, even if the distinction between gravitational and levitational had been taught ostensively—as the difference between the falling apple and the balloon. Philosophers are equally free to assert that 'we never really see a cat'. Take an unsophisticated person through the physicist's and the physiologist's story about perception, and 'then we don't really see *things*' is the form in which he will naturally express his bewilderment; it isn't just a philosopher's paradox. Similar considerations apply to 'things aren't really coloured'; 'I can't really be sure of anything'; 'I don't really have free will.'

This last instance has achieved a certain notoriety, thanks to Flew's treatment of it in his essay on 'Philosophy and Language'.[1] Flew draws attention to the fact that we have all learnt the use of the expression 'of his own free will',

[1] *Philosophical Quarterly*, 1955; reprinted in ed. A. G. N. Flew: *Essays in Conceptual Analysis*, 1956.

to cover such cases as that in which a bridegroom marries 'of his own free will'. So far so good. There are certainly circumstances in which we are accustomed to employ this expression. But we have also learnt criteria: we have been told that a person acts of his own free will only when his action proceeds from an act of will and when that act of will has the metaphysical peculiarity of being uncaused. If we wish to deny, as we well might, that this criterion is ever satisfied, then a natural way of expressing our conclusion is that 'there is no such thing as free will'. In a philosophical context we shall be quite well understood; nor will it follow that we shall no longer make such statements as that 'Hamlet returned to Denmark of his own free will but did not leave for England of his own free will'. But we shall have given notice, as it were, that this in no way commits us to accepting the conclusion that before he returned to Denmark he went through an uncaused act of will.

The paradigm case argument, then, does nothing to show that certain philosophical positions are 'absurd' or 'senseless'. At best, it serves to remind us—as, I suggested, the 'excluded opposite' argument may also remind us—that a philosopher's statements are not to be interpreted quite as a wholly unsophisticated person might interpret them. When Hippocrates denied that any disease was sacred, perhaps some innocent reader thought he was denying that anybody has ever suffered from epilepsy. Certainly if the bare statement 'there are no sacred diseases' were made out of its context, it could easily be ridiculed. 'Do you *really* mean that nobody ever suffers from fits, or rolls on the ground in a frenzy?' But our motto ought to be: 'Don't ask what a philosopher *could* mean; look and find out what he *did* mean'. If that is our motto we shall not find much use for paradigm case or excluded opposite **arguments.**

Chapter Seven

ALLOCATION TO CATEGORIES[1]

OUTSIDE philosophy, there are frequently disputes about how something, or some sort of thing, ought to be classified. The question might be raised whether *The Two Noble Kinsmen* is not after all a Shakespearean play; whether the flowering quince belongs to the genus *Cydonia*; whether a virus is a living organism. The answer may be not at all obvious. Shakespeare's plays differ so greatly in style, and the habit of collaboration was, at the time he wrote, so widespread, that it is very difficult to prove that Shakespeare had a hand, or what hand, in a particular play; the mechanisms of reproduction in a particular species of plant are often hard to determine; the behaviour of viruses is in some respects obscure.

In every case, empirical expertise is needed, whether in order to determine the characteristics of the thing in question, the general features of the class in which we are proposing to place it, or the utility of classifying it in a particular way. No philosophical argument can settle the matter—although, of course, general logical considerations about class-relationships will always be relevant.

Classificatory problems of this type can, in principle, arise within what has traditionally been regarded as a province of philosophy. Thus if right action is defined as action which is conducive to the happiness of the person towards whom it is directed, the question can be raised

[1] This chapter is very different in tone from its predecessors: it is tentative and exploratory. In those moments of truth which come to all men in the dark hours of the morning, I have often resolved to destroy it. But it will serve, I have persuaded myself, a useful function: illustrating what it is like to look for a philosophical argument, as distinct from employing more critically an argument which has already established its respectability.

whether, on this definition, truth-telling can be classified as a right action, i.e. whether it always makes people happier if we tell them the truth. This is purely an empirical issue, even if, in order to settle it, we need rely only on our general experience of human behaviour. More difficult questions of the same general sort are often felt to belong to casuistry rather than to ethics, since they require for their solution a considerable degree of practical wisdom or of theoretical knowledge. The more purely philosophical problems of ethics do not turn around this kind of difficulty, just as the philosophical problems of politics do not lie in the difficulty of classifying forms of government, or the philosophical problems of aesthetics in the difficulty of distinguishing between artistic genres.

Characteristically, indeed, the philosopher does not classify; he categorizes. To categorize he does not need to embark upon the elaborate empirical investigations of the biologist or the geologist; category-distinctions are established by philosophical reasoning, not by field-work. About so much, I imagine, there would be general agreement. The controversy arises when we try to distinguish, in a satisfactory way, between *belonging to a class* and *coming under a category*. Ordinary language is no help: 'category' is now an elegant variation of 'class'. Nor has philosophy established a firm technical use: if there is agreement that philosophy categorizes this is not accompanied by any parallel agreement about what are, and what are not, categorical distinctions.[1]

There seems, however, to be a measure of convergence

---

[1] Sometimes the categories are defined as levels, or orders, of existence; if the 'two-world' argument is valid, there are no such levels. Sometimes, they are defined as the forms of thought which, in thinking, we impose upon the world. This turns out to be a self-refuting theory: 'the world' must be thought—to enter into the theory—and yet cannot be thought, since it is that which is prior to thought. As for the view that the categories are 'conditions of existence', if this means that they are prior to but imposed upon existence, it breaks down, for two-world reasons; if it means, simply, that the categories are those predicates which things possess in virtue of existing it is the ontological version of my own, more formal, interpretation. In post-Hegelian writings, the word

on a certain number of cases: quality, relation, quantity, for example, would generally be regarded as categories. If those are typical, we notice at once an important, though negative, feature of categories. They are not modes of classifying kinds of things. Plants, animals, chemical substances, books, cannot be divided into those which are, and those which are not, describable in terms of qualities, relations or quantities. We can pick out of our shelves a set of books which are green, six in number and written by Shakespeare. So far, we employ the categories of quality, quantity, relation in our classifications. But we cannot classify books—or any other kind of thing—into those which permit, and those which do not permit, of being described by predicates which fall under those general categories.

Or so it would at first seem: but perhaps this is an illusion. Categories may, after all, be modes of classifying certain kinds of thing, although not every kind of thing. They may syntactically classify words and phrases. This is in many ways an attractive view. For one thing, it will have the consequence that the present chapter can be expeditiously completed. No special philosophical arguments will be needed in order to allocate to categories. Such a classification of words and phrases is a task for grammarians; grammarians have regular methods of determining into what syntactical classes words and phrases fall. Philosophers, if they wish to participate in the task of verbal classifications, should seek the grammarian's advice on what procedure to adopt.

Yet grammarians' conclusions have seldom satisfied philosophers. In the course of classifying sophistic fallacies,

---

'categories' is often used to refer to the most general concepts in a field of inquiry—the categories of physics, the categories of economics. There is no harm in this; if, indeed, the attempt to distinguish categories from classes should fail, it may turn out to be the only useful way of using the word. See also Manley Thompson 'On Category Differences' (*Phil. Rev.* Oct. 1957) and R. C. Cross 'Category Differences' (*Proc. Ar. Soc.* 1958-9).

Aristotle wrote as follows: 'Others [i.e. other fallacies] come about owing to the form of expression used . . . when a quality is expressed by a termination appropriate to a quantity, or vice versa, or what is active by a passive word, or a state by an active word. . . . For it is possible to use an expression to denote what does not belong to the class of actions at all as though it did so belong. Thus (e.g.) "thriving" is a word, which in the form of its expression is like "cutting" or "building"; yet the one denotes a certain quality—i.e. a certain condition—while the other denotes a certain action'.[1] Thus, Aristotle is suggesting, a purely syntactical division of predicates, one based on their grammatical form, need not correspond to a philosophical categorization.

Perhaps, however, one should say something like this: philosophical category-distinctions are simply a more refined version of the grammarian's classification-distinctions. If grammarians had been clever enough, or persistent enough, they would have noticed that 'thriving' is not grammatically parallel to 'cutting' or 'building'. Then, instead of classifying these three words together as 'present-participles'—or in addition to so doing—they would have distinguished 'thriving' as a state-word from 'cutting' and 'building' as action-words. Category-distinguishing is just a better way of doing grammar, much as systematic botany is a better way of doing what a horticulturalist does when he distinguishes flowers and plants from one another.

'Our investigation,' wrote Wittgenstein in *Philosophical Investigations*, 'is a grammatical one. Such an investigation sheds light on our problem by clearing misunderstandings away, misunderstandings concerning the use of words, caused, amongst other things, by certain analogies between the forms of expression in different regions of language' (§90). Clearly, however, it is one thing to say that philosophical investigations may be provoked by the realization that some ordinary grammatical classification is philo-

[1] *De Sophisticis Elenchis*, Chap. V, 166, trans. W. A. Pickard-Cambridge.

sophically misleading; quite another to say that the resulting investigation is itself grammatical. 'Some of them [i.e. the misunderstandings] can be removed,' Wittgenstein continues, 'by substituting one form of expression for another.' But such substitutions may completely alter the grammatical form of a sentence; the mere fact that such a method is appropriate suggests that it is not grammar which is interesting us.

When, furthermore, the grammarian uses his subject as an instrument of correction, it is because somebody has said 'Between you and I', not because he has maintained that 'pleasure is a process' or 'good is a quality'. Neither of these sentences, on the face of it, is ungrammatical; neither of them is either an accurate or an inaccurate description of the way 'good' or 'pleasure' functions grammatically in sentences.

According to Carnap, however,[1] this is only because 'pleasure is a process' and 'good is a quality' are misleadingly expressed, in the 'material' as distinct from the 'formal' mode. 'Pleasure is a process' should be reformulated as ' "Pleasure" is a process-word' and 'good is a quality' should be reformulated as ' "good" is a quality-word'. This done, the statements would appear in their true, syntactical, light, and we should be left in no doubt how their truth or falsity is to be decided—by reference to the rules of syntax.

In fact, however, translation into the formal mode leaves us with no way whatever of settling the original issues. We could easily enough determine, no doubt, whether it is true that in English 'good' is used as an adjective. But this does not settle the matter unless, in despite of Aristotle and his successors, we are willing to accept as unquestionable the *prima facie* categorial suggestions of grammar. No philosopher has ever denied that 'good' is sometimes an adjective; and if 'quality-word' does not mean 'adjective' but

---

[1] When he wrote *The Logical Syntax of Language*. See, for example, pp. 298 and 311 in the English translation (1937).

rather 'word which refers to a quality' then the alleged translation into the formal mode does not solve, but only begs, the philosophical issue. As for 'process-word' what does this mean, if not 'verb'? Surely Plato, when he suggested that 'pleasure is a process' knew quite well that 'pleasure' is not a verb!

If the existence or non-existence of a grammatical distinction does not settle a philosophical category-debate, it is equally true that the outcome of a philosophical debate need have no effect whatever on the writings of grammarians. When Kant wrote in *The Critique of Pure Reason* (A598) of 'the illusion which is caused by the confusion of a logical within a real predicate (that is, with a predicate which determines a thing)', he was not exhorting grammarians to divide predicates into 'logical' and 'real' predicates—that is not the sort of distinction they could make or ever need to make. For them, the sentence: 'Romantic love is an illusion' is parallel in all respects to 'Romantic love is a nuisance'—and Kant is not trying to correct them. Nor is Russell when he denies that 'the king of France' is 'the real subject' of 'the king of France is bald' anticipating that children will no longer be taught to pick out 'the king of France' as the subject of that sentence. Indeed, it is part of his object to *contrast* the 'real' with the 'grammatical' subject.

A question remains, however—and the difficulty in answering it is the motive-force behind the attempt to regard philosophy as a species of grammar—'If philosophical category-problems are not grammatical problems, what else can they be? How can they be settled, if not by the close and systematic study of idiom?' That is the problem which now lies before us. The most general answer is that the supposition that a description belongs to one category rather than to another leads to inadmissible consequences. (I use the word 'inadmissible' to cover consequences which are either false, self-contradictory or 'absurd'.) As it stands, however, this answer will not serve to differentiate a category-distinguishing argument from a classification-argument. For the ascription to Shakespeare of *The Two Noble Kinsmen* is rejected on the ground that a certain conclusion which would follow from that ascription—the conclusion that Shakespeare could write plays which lack psychological insight—is false. So if the general thesis is to stand, that to categorize is not to classify, we shall have to show that the argument to inadmissibility is, in the case of category-allocations, of a special sort, philosophical in character.

Aristotle saw that the dialectic of the Sophists depended, in large part, on category-confusions. In a dialogue like the *Euthydemus*, similarly, Plato exhibits the sophistical method, considered as a kind of play, as something which largely consists in the mis-allocations of predicates to categories. He, and Aristotle, pointed to category-distinctions by drawing our attention to the sophistical fallacies which result from erroneous categorizations.

Thus, in the *Euthydemus*, Socrates sums up part of Euthydemus' argument as follows: 'Do you mean to say that inasmuch as it is impossible for the same thing to be and also not to be, it follows that since I know one thing, I know all, for I cannot both be knowing and not knowing at the same time?' (293, Jowett translation). Euthydemus has presumed, that is, that 'knowing' is categorially parallel to 'laughing'; that since it is impossible for the same thing to be at the same time both laughing and not laughing, so equally it must be impossible for the same thing at the same time to be both knowing and not knowing. But then it will follow that to know anything we must know everything, since otherwise we can at the same time be knowing (something) and yet not knowing (something else).

One can use this Sophistic argument—Socrates in his side-remarks suggests as much—not as a mere piece of dialectical play, but as a way of drawing attention to the fact that 'knowing' does not belong to the same category as 'laughing'. The argument, thus re-disposed, falls into

two stages. The first consists in drawing a formal consequence which follows if 'knowing' is categorially parallel
to 'laughing', viz. that 'nobody can both know and not
know'. The second consists in arguing that this proposition
cannot be true, for if it were we could not know anything
unless we know everything.

As it happens, there are purely philosophical objections
to the assertion that 'if we know anything, we know
everything'. Let 'knowing anything' be represented by
KA, and 'knowing everything' by KE. Then KE involves
knowing that if KA, KE. But then it must also include
knowing that KE includes knowing that if KA, KE; so
KA involves knowing that KE includes knowing that if
KA, KE. But then KE must include knowing that KA
involves knowing that KE includes knowing that if KA,
KE. So there is generated an infinite regress; we could
never know anything if this involved knowing everything.

This is the strongest form of category-allocation argument—to a consequence which is inadmissible for philosophical reasons: the kind of argument which philosophers
naturally seek to construct. In the *Euthydemus*, however,
Plato is content to suggest that it would be *empirically false*
to assert that if anyone knows anything he knows everything, and this seems to be sufficient to make the category-
point. We might describe this as the 'weaker' form of the
category-allocation argument, but it is still strong enough
to do the job. So it does not seem to be the case that a
category-allocation argument always has to issue in conclusions which are inadmissible for logical or philosophical
reasons, as distinct from simply being false. The major
point is that the category-allocation argument is still not
an ordinary classification argument, even when it issues in
a conclusion which is empirically false rather than logically
objectionable. For a category-allocation argument passes
through a formal phase—the phase in which a certain
formal consequence of supposing that a predicate belongs
to a certain category is brought out. The argument which

allocates 'laughing' and 'knowing' to different categories
is not an attempt to prove that 'laughing things' and
'things that know' belong to different classes. 'Laughing'
belongs to a different category from 'knowing', even if it be
true that all laughing things, and only laughing things, know.

Nor does the argument seem to be grammatical; it does
not set out to prove that 'knowing' is not a participle. It
begins, certainly, from a grammatical fact; or, rather, the
category-confusion which the argument seeks to dispel is
made plausible by such a fact. One can, in English, on
certain occasions use the expression 'Either he knows or he
does not know'; this grammatical fact may mislead us into
supposing that what we are on such an occasion asserting
is logically parallel to 'Either he laughs or he does not
laugh'. In French, the idiom does not exist: if English were
like French, one would be obliged to say 'Either you know
or you do not know *it*' and so the confusing grammatical
parallelism would not exist.

It is, then, a fact about the English language that it contains categorially-misleading forms of speech. One does not,
all the same, discover that these forms of speech are confusing by a closer examination of our linguistic habits; on
the contrary, one has to work out the consequences of
taking their *prima facie* categorial suggestions seriously.
What establishes, furthermore, that there is a certain
category-distinction is not some fact about the English
language, although in some languages no one would feel
the need of establishing it. It is a peculiarity of English
that 'I know' can be a complete sentence; it is a peculiarity
of French that 'Je sais' cannot be a complete sentence. It is
not a peculiarity of any language, or a characteristic of all
languages, that knowing is a relation. 'Knowledge is a
relation' does not assert either that 'Things that know fall
into the class of relations' or that ' "Knowledge" is a
relation-word'; what it says is that in '*x* knows', 'knows'
describes *x* in a relational way.

It might be suggested, however, that what 'Knowledge

is a relation' means is something like this: 'In an ideal language knowledge *would be* a relation-word'. That is what Carnap at one time wanted to maintain. No doubt he was so far right, that in a language which did not mislead us about categories all categorial distinctions would be syntactically marked. (This is not a mere identity; it brings out the fact that categories càn be indicated in the syntax of a language; we are categorially misled by our grammar only because our grammar generally makes categories clear to us.) But it does not follow that we can determine what category-distinctions to make by considering what would happen in an ideal language. On the contrary, in order to work out the structure of an ideal language, we have first to determine what category-distinctions to make. If we are puzzled whether good is a quality or a relation, we cannot resolve our puzzlement by asking how it would be represented in an ideal language; we can decide how it would be represented in such a language only after we know whether it is a relation or quality. This, we have suggested, can only be settled by argument, which involves considerations of a formal-logical kind.

As another example, consider the sophistical argument which runs as follows: 'The Planets are seven in number, Mars and Venus are planets: therefore, Mars and Venus are seven in number.' This argument can be used as a way of bringing out the lack of categorial parallelism between the predicates 'seven in number' and 'large in size'. From the proposition 'The planets are large in size', it can be concluded, in virtue of the fact that Mars and Venus are planets, that 'Mars and Venus are large in size'; from 'the planets are seven in number' it cannot be concluded, in virtue of the same fact, that 'Mars and Venus are seven in number'. Yet in both cases the premises are true, and the argument is parallel in form; so there must be something wrong with the supposition that, as grammar suggests, 'large in size' and 'seven in number' are categorially parallel.

A very similar argument is used by Frege in *The Foundations of Arithmetic* (trans. J. L. Austin, 40e–41e). Whereas, he points out, we can combine 'Solon was wise' and 'Thales was wise' into 'Solon and Thales were wise', we cannot argue that 'Solon was one' and 'Thales was one', so 'Solon and Thales were one'. 'But,' he continues, 'it is hard to see why that should be impossible, if "one" were a property both of Solon and Thales in the same way that "wise" is'. We can sum up thus: whereas 'Solon was wise, Thales was wise, therefore Thales and Solon were wise' leads from true premises to a true conclusion, this is not the case in 'Thales was one, Solon was one, so Thales and Solon were one'. Here the conclusion is inadmissible; yet the premises are true, and the form of the arguments is apparently identical. What must be wrong, therefore, is the assumption that 'one' and 'wise' belong to the same category.

There seems to be a general connexion, then, between seeing to what category a predicate belongs and seeing what kinds of logical work can be carried out with premises which contain it. We are led to distinguish between relational and qualitative predicates, when we come to see that, as the Eleatic Stranger expresses the matter in Plato's *Sophist* (256b), 'We must admit without grumbling the statement that motion is the same and not the same; for when we apply these expressions to it, our point of view is different' i.e. that it can truly be said of the one thing that it both is and is not 'the same', whereas it cannot truly be said that it both is and is not red. Similarly we are led to distinguish between numerical and qualitative predicates by considering the sort of confusion into which the Sophists fall, or the sort of argument which Frege deliberately constructed.

When, on the other hand, there is disagreement about what is and what is not an inadmissible conclusion, we soon reach a category-impasse. Ethics and aesthetics provide notable examples of such impasses; they can be illustrated from Nowell-Smith's *Ethics* (pp. 72–3). Nowell-

Smith begins by bringing out differences between the predicates 'being a weed' and 'being a carnation'. We could put his points thus: (1) No plant can be both a carnation and not a carnation, but it is not true that no plant can be both a weed, and not a weed: many plants are weeds in Australia but not in England; (2) There is a set of properties the possession of which is sufficient and necessary for 'being a carnation', i.e. there are propositions 'this is Pr_1, Pr_2', where Pr_1, Pr_2 are properties, from which it follows that 'this is a carnation'. There are no such propositions from which 'this is a weed' can be deduced.

Then Nowell-Smith tries to apply to ethical predicates this general method of distinguishing predicates, in order to show that ethical predicates fall into the (relational) category of weeds. But the difficulty is that in the ethical case there is no agreement whether conditions (1) and (2) are satisfied. Some moral theorists affirm, but others deny, that 'No act can be both good and not good'; some affirm, and some deny, that 'X is good' follows, or could follow, from a set of propositions which ascribe qualities to X. So there is not that level of agreement which enables us to decide that 'X is a weed' is not parallel to 'X is a carnation'. Nowell-Smith has rightly drawn attention to the fact that if the possession of certain qualities is necessary for being good, then it will be self-contradictory to assert that something is good but has not these qualities. Whether it is self-contradictory, however, is precisely the point at issue. The category-allocation argument has in this case been carried only to the first of two stages—the stage of formal development; the difficulty still remains of carrying it through its second stage, the stage of showing that this formal development leads to inadmissible conclusions.

We are all prepared to agree that 'either we know everything or we know nothing' is an inadmissible conclusion, so that if this conclusion follows (via 'either we know or we don't know') from regarding 'knowing' as parallel to 'laughing', there can in fact be no such parallelism. There is no such point of agreement in ethics and aesthetics; no generally inadmissible conclusion seems to follow from the assertion, or the denial, that 'nothing can be both good and not-good'. But anyhow, the attempt to draw such conclusions by way of a *formal* development is the only possible way of bringing out what is involved in the category-dispute.

On the whole, philosophers have had very little to say about the process of category-allocation. Aristotle presumes, rightly enough, that we shall simply *see* that 'thriving' is different from 'cutting' as soon as our attention is drawn to the fact. He does not put the difference formally, as we might, by pointing out that from 'x is cutting' it follows that 'there is a y, such that y is being cut', whereas from 'x is thriving' it does not follow that 'there is a y, such that y is being thrived'. Nor does he consider, in general, what steps we are to take in the event of a disagreement about category-allocation.

Ryle, indeed, is one of the first philosophers to devote any considerable attention to category-allocation arguments. In his article on 'Categories',[1] he suggests that two expressions differ in category if there are sentence-frames of the form '. . . is a Pr' such that one expression can, and the other cannot, fit into such frames. Take, for example, the sentence-frame '. . . is in bed'. We can without absurdity substitute for the dotted gap any name of a person—John, William, Mary—but not the days of the week. So 'John' and 'Saturday' belong to different categories.

In employing this method, Ryle is supposing that *things* belong to different categories. On the other hand, I have been proceeding on the assumption that no kind of thing comes under one category rather than another—so that, say, 'persons' and 'days of the week' would, on the view I have been taking, belong to different *classes* but not to different *categories*. On Ryle's view, indeed, the members

[1] *Proc. Ar. Soc.*, 1937–8, reprinted in A. Flew: *Logic and Language*, Vol. II, 1953.

of any two mutually exclusive classes would automatically belong to different categories. For it is always possible, in the case of any two mutually exclusive kinds of thing, to construct sentences such that one can, and the other cannot, appear without absurdity as the subject of such sentences. Let the kinds of thing be X and Y, and the sentence-frame be '. . . is not an X'. Then Y, but not X, can without absurdity appear as the subject in such a sentence.[1] Therefore, on Ryle's view, X and Y belong to different categories.

Perhaps, however this conclusion—which seems wholly to destroy the distinction between classes and categories—can be avoided by a slight modification. Let us say that two expressions belong to different categories only if there is a diversified range of sentences in which one can, and the other cannot, without absurdity appear. The immediate difficulty, of course, is that expressions like 'a diversified range of cases' are not precise. On the face of it, however, there is a wide range of such sentences in the case of most mutually exclusive classes, so that even this modified position will not permit us to distinguish classes from categories.

Take, for example, a chop and the plate it rests upon. A chop can be, and a plate cannot be, tasty, succulent, juicy; boiled, grilled or roasted; underdone or overdone; tough or tender; fresh or stale; gristly or fatty; it can be a pork chop, a mutton chop, or a lamb chop; you can treat it with preservative, bone it, or macerate it . . . and yet if a chop and a plate belong to different categories, the distinction between categories and classes looks tenuous indeed. So it does not seem that, even after revision, Ryle's method will differentiate between classification-distinctions and category-distinctions. We can arrive at absurd propositions by mis-classifications. This is concealed only by the fact that no one ever does mis-classify a plate as a chop.

A rather different line of reasoning is what Ryle has

[1] Presuming that 'X is not an X' is 'absurd'; if not, the cases adduced in J.J.C. Smart: 'A Note on Categories' (*Br. Jnl. Phil. Science*, 1953) will suffice to establish my point.

called 'the argument from the non-transferability of epithets'. This argument Ryle traces back to Aristotle's *Nicomachean Ethics* where it is directed against Plato's suggestion in the *Philebus* that 'pleasure is a process'.[1] Aristotle argues, in effect, that if pleasure were a process it would have to *take time*. It would then be sensible to ask concerning a pleasure such questions as 'Did you get half-way through being pleased?' questions which in fact have no application. A person is either pleased or displeased; he can be interrupted half-way through a pleasant dinner but not half-way through being pleased. Wittgenstein in *The Blue Book* raises a similar objection to the view that 'knowing how to go on' is a process: 'What sort of process is this *knowing how to go on?*' he writes. 'Ask yourself "how long does it take to know how to go on?" Or is it an instantaneous process?' (p. 40). In Ryle's *The Concept of Mind* arguments of this sort play a considerable part. Thus, for example, in discussing the view that happiness is a feeling, Ryle writes: 'Feelings, in any strict sense, are things that come and go or wax and wane in a few seconds; they stab or they grumble; we feel them all over us or else in a particular part. The victim may say that he keeps on having tweaks, or that they come only at fairly long intervals. No one would describe his happiness or discontentment in any such terms' (p. 100).

Does such an argument differ in any important respect from an empirical classification argument? Suppose somebody were to assert that the sort of headaches which are normally described as organic are all in fact neurotic. Then he might be met with the following argument: 'Neurotic headaches come and go; they are referred now to this, now to that, part of the head; the patient uses expressions like these: "My head feels tight"; "Something seems to have snapped", and so on. An organic headache is not described in these terms'. Formally, this seems to be exactly parallel

---

[1] Cf. Ryle's 'Proofs in Philosophy', *Revue Internationale de Philosophie*, No. 27–28, 1954, p. 6.

to Ryle's argument. It is true that, if Ryle is correct, the classification-mistakes of philosophers are of a peculiarly egregious sort—rather as if someone were seriously to suppose that a plate is a kind of chop—but mis-classification mistakes they none the less are.

At least, this is so in the case of 'happiness is a kind of feeling'. 'Pleasure is a process', however, is in a rather different position—for 'process' has at least some claim to be a category: every kind of thing, one might well suggest, is describable in terms of the processes in which it participates. Now if 'process' is used in a categorial way, there is a formal argument by which a process can be distinguished from a state. Consider such processes as eating, drinking, writing, cutting, building, pushing, pulling. Then in each case from 'x is engaged in such-and-such a process' it follows that 'there is a y which is being processed (eaten, written, pushed) by x'. From 'x is pleased' (contented, wet, rusty, etc.) it does not, however, follow that 'there is a y such that y is being pleased by x'. The difference between process and state may not always be grammatically obvious. For example, in English, we use the sentence 'He is sitting down' to express either a process or a state. But a number of European languages bring out the contrast, by talking, in the process-case, of a person as 'sitting *himself* down', as distinct from, in the case of the state, 'being seated'. So in this instance, too, there is in the process-case something that is being sat down—although usually this is *myself*. (I am not suggesting, of course, that whenever there is such a converse argument there is a process; but only that this is necessary for being a process).

A difficulty now begins to emerge, which I have so far been deliberately avoiding. I have written as if it were clear what was meant by a 'formal' consideration and a 'formal' argument. Now that converse relations—as distinct from contradictions, syllogisms and the like—have come into the picture, that assumption begins to look more dubious. Consider the Aristotle-Ryle argument about pleasure. One might put it thus: 'If pleasure is a process, then there must be a rate x which is the rate at which pleasure proceeds'. Why isn't this quite as formal as 'If pleasure is a process, there must be an x which is being processed?' If that, in turn, isn't formal, why is it less formal than 'If red is a quality, x is either red or not red?' Or consider such a case as this: a boy, on an afternoon dedicated to compulsory games, goes for a ramble. Rebuked by his sports-master, he claims that rambling is a game, and is met with the reply, 'Rambling cannot be a game, because a game is something you can win or lose, and you can't win or lose at rambling.' In other words, 'if rambling is a game, there must be a person x who is the victor in rambling'. Why shouldn't this be regarded as a formal argument which establishes membership of the games-category? Why, equally, shouldn't we say that 'man' is a category, on the ground that if Tom is a man, there must be a true proposition of the form: 'there is a time t, such that Tom was born at this time?'

So, it might be said, to cut off category-allocations from classifications, on the ground that the first has to be established by way of a purely formal stage whereas the second does not, would be question-begging. There are various ways of meeting this criticism. One is to accept it, and then to say that although there is some convenience in talking about categories, or formal concepts, at one end of a continuum, and about classes, or empirical concepts, at the other end, still there is a continuum. Categories are nothing but very general classes, formal concepts are nothing but unusually non-discriminating empirical concepts.[1] Another way is to try to stop the slide at a certain point, e.g. by

[1] Compare the definition of category in John of St. Thomas. 'A category is nothing else than a series or arrangement of superior and inferior predicates, starting with a supreme genus which is predicated of every inferior, and ending with the individual, which is subject to every superior' (*Material Logic*, trans. Y. R. Simon *et al.*, p. 184). On this view, to say that something belongs to category x is to say that it belongs to a system of classification in which x is the supreme genus.

drawing a line at some point just above 'being a process'. A 'process', it might be argued, is an empirically describable type of relation. 'Process' and 'state' can be formally distinguished in virtue of the fact that they are relations and qualities, respectively, but they can also be empirically distinguished as being different forms of empirical predicates. (Just as 'red' and 'larger' can be categorially distinguished as quality and relation, but also empirically distinguished as a colour and a size-comparison.) What W. E. Johnson called 'determinables' may fall into a third group between categories and classes.

The general tendency of Ryle's argument has been towards the continuum-approach, but all the same he wants to draw the line somewhere; he wants to talk about 'category-mistakes' as something different from 'misclassifications'. I have already suggested that his category-test would not in fact enable him to distinguish classes from categories. But we may, all the same, profitably examine certain of the category-mistakes he alleges; they are not category-mistakes, as we have defined category-mistakes, but we may well be reluctant to call them misclassifications, either.

In *The Concept of Mind* (p. 16) Ryle introduces the conception of a category-mistake by describing the behaviour of a foreign visitor to Oxford or Cambridge. Shown colleges, the playing fields, the administrative offices, he is still not satisfied; he wants to see the *University*. 'His mistake,' Ryle writes, 'lay in his innocent assumption that it was correct to speak of Christ Church, the Bodleian Library, the Ashmolean Museum *and* the University, to speak, that is, as if "the University" stood for an extra member of the class of which these other units are members. He was mistakenly allocating the University to the same category as that to which the other institutions belong.'

We can compare the foreigner's mistake with another mistake to which Cambridge freshmen are said to be prone; pointing to the offices of the Cambridge University Press, they ask, 'What College is that?' Their error would naturally be described as a mis-classification : the innocent freshmen have wrongly supposed that the Press-building belongs to the class of College-buildings. On the other hand, when Ryle's foreigner asks to be shown 'the University' he is not merely supposing that the University, too, is a building—this would be an ordinary mis-classification; he is failing to realize that he has already been shown the University, that the University is the whole of which what he has been shown are the parts.

Ryle's examples all involve a part-whole confusion, but the same situation can arise when there is a species-genus confusion. Suppose that same foreigner were to visit Australia. We show him a kangaroo, a koala, a wombat . . . and he says: 'Very interesting. But what I should really like to see is a marsupial'. Then this is a rather different mistake from the mistake which we would have made had we pointed to a kangaroo and said: 'There's a koala'. Our zoologically ignorant pupil is wrongly supposing that a marsupial is another member of the class of which koalas, wombats, kangaroos are members, when in fact it *is* that class. One might well wish to give a mistake of that kind a special name, on the ground that 'mis-classification' suggests the kangaroo-koala, or the Press-College, sort of mistake, rather than the 'Show me a marsupial', 'Where is the University?' kind of mistake. But it does not seem to be a mistake of any special philosophical interest. It rests on an ignorance of empirical fact: a failure to realize that a College is part of a University, or that a kangaroo is a species of marsupial. If Ryle's foreign visitor happens to be a philosopher, we shall not think any the worse of his philosophical abilities merely because he does not know that the Colleges form part of the University. When he learns that in fact they do, he will not have made a philosophical advance.

But when Frege drew attention to the difference between predicates like 'one' and predicates like 'wise' he *was* making a philosophical advance, and we *shall* think worse of a philosopher who says that 'good is a quality' and then goes on to identify 'being good' with 'being liked'. Perhaps we need a special name for exceptionally egregious classification-mistakes, those which do not consist in wrongly believing that something is a member of a certain species, but in wrongly believing that what is really the genus to which certain species belong is co-ordinate with those species; there might be the same, or a different, name for a similar mistake about parts and wholes. But 'category-mistakes' suggests an error of a peculiarly philosophical sort, whereas in these mistakes no more is involved than a formidable degree of empirical ignorance.

If my line of argument has any force, Ryle is drawing attention in *The Concept of Mind*, not to a single sort of confusion—a 'category-mistake'—but to a number of quite different forms of confusion. Some of them may well be category-mistakes, in my sense of the phrase, as when, for example, Ryle sets out to show that certain philosophical ways of talking about mind rest on a confusion between dispositions and occurrences. At other times, he is rejecting a traditional classification, as in denying that happiness is a kind of feeling; at still other times, he is arguing that if when we have had displayed to us a great range of mental behaviour and achievements, our response is: 'Very interesting, but now tell me about the mind', we are behaving exactly like the innocent foreigner.

Ryle would particularly object to the suggestion, made above, that in order to distinguish between mis-classifications and mis-allocations of categories we might need to reduce, rather, than to extend, the list of categories we are at first inclined to draw up; even the traditional list, as it appears, say, in Aristotle, he describes as 'intolerably exiguous' (*Dilemmas*, p. 10). But whether it is exiguous depends, of course, on what we wish to do with categories.

The classification of animals into vertebrate and invertebrate would be 'intolerably exiguous' if that were the only division the biologist was prepared to make, but it is still a very important biological fact that some animals possess, and others lack, a backbone. If one thinks of the categories as general modes of description, applicable to a thing of any sort, it will not be surprising if they turn out to be few in number. Let us suppose that of every thing, we know that it has qualities, that it stands in relations to other things, that it acts and is acted upon, that it exists in various states. Any description of it, if this were a complete list, would be a description of its qualities, its relations, its modes of action, what influences it, what state it is in. But this would still leave open the question whether it is animal, mineral or vegetable, terrestrial or celestial, alkaline or inspirational, depressed or liquid. The pigeonholes would be infinite—although they would only come in a limited number of shapes.

There is, then, no general objection to the supposition that there is a limited number of categories—as distinct from the objection that there are modes of description which will not fit into any of a proposed list of categories. This latter is a matter which can only be settled by the use of allocation-arguments. Whether the list is large or small does not at all concern us; the difficulty, rather, is that the attempt to distinguish categories from classes by formal-logical means turns out to depend upon a prior distinction between the formal and the non-formal: on our being able to say that it follows *formally*, from the fact that a process is a relation, that whenever someone is engaged in a process, there must be something he is processing, whereas it is not a formal consequence of pleasure's being a process that it proceeds at a certain rate.

Indeed, three difficult distinctions turn out to be intricately inter-related; the distinctions between category and class, the formal and the non-formal, the absurd and the false. Such an inter-relation of problems is characteristic of philosophy; to bring it out—to make our commitments clearer to us—is one of the main objects of philosophical reasoning. That is true, of course, of inquiry of every sort; it draws attention to unexpected consequences of commitments. Russell once suggested—and if he did not himself practise what he preached, some of his contemporaries at least tried to do so—that philosophers, instead of working on a large canvas, should go in search of 'piece-meal, detailed and verifiable results'. But in fact philosophical results never are piece-meal; to 'verify' them we must take account of their wider philosophical consequences. One cannot simply ignore the fact that, say, a particular analysis of perception involves a two-world ontology; this would be like ignoring the fact that a particular analysis of 'chemical bonds' is inconsistent with the electronic theory of matter. With this difference: in science, as soon as the scientist is confronted by two incompatible propositions, p and q, he generally knows, or can rapidly find out, which of the two propositions to reject; in philosophy this is not the case. No doubt, the difference is one of degree only. The scientist does not always know what to do, when he is confronted by the fact that a theory to which he is inclined seems to lead to a conclusion which he does not wish to accept; in philosophy, there is sometimes no doubt what is to be done. But the difference in degree is none the less an important one, and largely accounts for the relative difficulty in settling philosophical questions.

Consider the present instance. Roughly speaking, I have suggested that predicates Pr_1, Pr_2 belong to different categories if a formal development based on a true proposition 'x is Pr_1' leads to a true conclusion whereas a parallel formal development based on 'x is Pr_2' leads to an inadmissible conclusion. Ryle, on the other hand, has suggested that X, Y belong to different categories if absurdities result from substituting X for Y in propositions of the form 'Y is Z'. Criticizing Ryle, I drew attention to cases where, so I said, X, Y belong to the same category yet absurdity results from substituting X for Y; he might well reply that Pr_1, Pr_2 can belong to different categories in cases where, on my restricted concept of 'formality', the arguments derived from 'x is Pr_1' and leading to true conclusions would be formally parallel to the arguments derived from 'x is Pr_2' and leading to true conclusions. Then deeper conflicts arise: how to determine whether two arguments are 'formally parallel', how to distinguish between falsity and absurdity. How, if at all, we must now ask ourselves, can disputes of this sort be settled? Is philosophical reasoning in the end powerless?

Consider first the case of 'absurdity'. Take the following sentences:

(1) My kangaroo is green
(2) My kangaroo is good at arithmetic
(3) My kangaroo is the fifth day of the week
(4) My kangaroo is not a kangaroo.

If some critical reader wishes to reject (1), then he will naturally, and without fear of being misunderstood, describe it as 'false'. (Presuming, only, that he believes that in fact I own a kangaroo.) But if he were to describe (2) as false, this would leave open the possibility that he thought that some kangaroos, although not mine, were good at arithmetic. So he might rather reply: 'That's absurd—a kangaroo can't be good at arithmetic—or bad at it either'. As for (3), his natural presumption would be that I was mad, did not understand English, had made a slip of the tongue, or was asserting, in a ridiculously circumlocutory way, that my pet's name is 'Thursday'. In the case of (4), the everyday interpretation, no doubt, would be that although I had always described my pet as a kangaroo it is not in fact a kangaroo, but, say, a wallaby. In a logic book, however, such a sentence would be read as an example of a 'logically false' or 'self-contradictory', proposition.

Until recently, most philosophers have concentrated almost all their attention upon cases like (1) and cases like

(4), in its logic-book interpretation. This is natural enough. Two forms of human enterprise have attracted the attention of philosophers: mathematics and empirical science.[1] Scientific arguments make use of sentences like (1), mathematical arguments make use of sentences like (4). On the other hand, sentences like (2) only appear in fiction and sentences like (3) in the ravings of lunatics and the wilder effusions of poets.

There is, on the face of it, a yawning gulf between (1) and (4); so long as we concentrate on such sentences we feel that we have a firm grasp of the difference between empirical and logical falsity. But the intervention of (2) and (3) disturbs us. Are they empirically or logically false? Never having had to consider the matter, we do not know what to say.

A number of possibilities confront us: not only in the mathematical sense that a variety of different combinations can be constructed out of a list of four items, but in the sense that many of these combinations attract philosophical adherents. Some philosophers—most recently, the followers of Wittgenstein—like to distinguish; they are very likely to say that each item in the list has its own type of falsity, giving them such names as accidental empirical falsity, necessary empirical falsity, grammatical falsity, logical falsity, in order to mark the differences. Generalizers, on the contrary, are likely to deny that there is any important distinction involved; each item on the list, they might say, is empirically false, although some more obviously so than others. (Quine and other contemporary American philosophers have sometimes written as if this were their view.) Traditional formalists will wish to distinguish sharply between 'That kangaroo is not a

[1] This is true, at least, both in the Greek and the modern periods. Some mediaeval philosophers were more interested in e.g. fables. So there is a quite elaborate discussion of absurdity in John of Salisbury's *Metalogicon* (Ch. 15–18). It is there associated with a theory of types. John sees the difficulty of drawing any sharp distinction between the absurd, the unconventional, the poetical, and the false.

kangaroo', read as self-contradictory, and all the other sentences in the list, which are, they would say, empirically false, even if some of them are so obviously false that nobody would be tempted to utter them seriously. Ryle is suggesting, I take it, that (3) and (4) should be grouped together, as being absurd for logical reasons; what he would say about (2) is not so clear. The basic difference between (2) and (3) is that whereas kangaroos and things which are good at arithmetic have a great many relatively specific predicates in common, kangaroos and days of the week have only the most general characteristics in common (This comes out in the fact that we 'can picture' or 'can imagine' a kangaroo being good at arithmetic). So a philosopher might well wish to maintain that there are three groups: the empirically false (1), the 'absurd' (2) and (3), and the logically false (4). In the earlier writings of logical positivism, such a mode of classification is sometimes suggested.

Similarly, suppose we are confronted by the following set of arguments:

(1) If no kangaroos are carnivorous, then nothing carnivorous is a kangaroo

(2) If a kangaroo is taller than a wallaby, then a wallaby is shorter than a kangaroo

(3) If a wallaby is shorter than a kangaroo, it can pass under that gate

(4) If a kangaroo is a marsupial, the female genital tract must be doubled

(5) If kangaroos live in Australia, they must be hardy.

Once again, a gulf seems to yawn between (1) and (5), but the interpolation of (2), (3), (4) disturbs our intuitive grasp of the distinction between the formal and the nonformal. We might feel inclined to suggest that in each case the connexion is empirical, or that this is true in all cases except (1) to (3) or. . . . Exactly the same situation arises in regard to categories and classes. Our intuitive feeling that we know the difference between the two is disturbed by contemplation of the series:

(1) Jones is a man
(2) Red is a colour
(3) Pleasure is a process
(4) Knowledge is a relation

Does only (4) allocate to a category? Or do both (3) and (4)? Or do all four allocate to a class? Or does (2) bring red under a 'determinable' whereas (3) brings pleasure under an 'empirical', as distinct from a 'formal', category?

By now the conventionalist will have lost patience. There is one way, and one way only, of settling such a dispute, he will say: arbitrary decision. For some purposes it is convenient to draw distinctions, for other purposes it is better to ignore distinctions; for some purposes the distinctions are best made at a certain point, for other purposes at a different point. In the end, and not very far from the beginning, philosophical reasoning gets us nowhere: all it does is to confuse us, by making what is really a decision-problem look as if it were a theoretical problem, thus intolerably complicating what ought to be a simple choice.

Undoubtedly, conventionalism has a good deal to be said for it. Often enough, one must admit, decisions have been confusingly disguised as deductions; what distinctions we bother to make will certainly depend upon our interests and concerns; if we distinguish sharply between categories and classes, the false and the absurd, the valid and the true, we shall always, in some degree, be deciding to use words in a way in which they are not ordinarily used, and so far 'establishing a new convention'. Conventionalism, too, promises us liberation from an endless metaphysical treadmill, in which we establish differences by using a criterion, and then find that to justify the use of that criterion we need to make another differentiation which we do not know how to make. An act of choice, it might seem—

'here I draw the line'—is the only way of establishing a secure starting-point.

The difficulty, however, is that we have to distinguish not only cases but classes of cases, and this resuscitates our original problem. If we say—'I intend to describe as "logically false" all sentences like, and only sentences like, "my kangaroo is not a kangaroo" '—we shall have to determine, and this was really our original difficulty, what sentences are like 'My kangaroo is not a kangaroo'. 'My kangaroo is green' is like 'my kangaroo is not a kangaroo' in containing 'my kangaroo' and 'is', but it would be ridiculous to describe it as being logically false.

Perhaps, however, we should work with lists, we should simply lay it down that certain signs are formal constants, and that logically false propositions contain one or the other of such-and-such combinations of constants. 'No satisfactory criterion for distinguishing just what is logic from what is not', writes Nelson Goodman, 'has been discovered. Rather, logic is specified by listing the signs and principles that are to be called logical: and the lists given by different logicians are not all the same'.[1] Should I then just say that such-and-such is not a category, just say that such-and-such are not formal consequences, just say (in criticizing Ryle) that such-and-such propositions are not absurd, but false? And if challenged, point to my list of categories, my list of formal consequences, my list of absurd propositions? The last case brings out an obvious difficulty: listing is only possible in certain special instances, where we are convinced that no new candidates could possibly arise; clearly, we could list the absurd propositions only if we identified them with logically false propositions and these in turn with propositions containing certain logical constants and certain patterns of variables.

Quite apart from that practical difficulty, however, a merely arbitrary classification would be quite pointless. It would be quite useless to draw up a list of classes and a list

[1] 'About', *Mind*, Jan. 1961, p. 8.

of categories if one merely decided arbitrarily what was to go in each list. In the case of logic, conventionalism has been used as an instrument of conservativism; there is an established subject—formal logic—and its integrity has been preserved by defining it as being concerned with those signs and principles with which it has traditionally been concerned. But the effect of this is to hinder inquiry, not to advance it, if there are, or could be, other signs or principles which will generate the same type of theoretical construction; if not, the signs and principles ought to be definable in virtue of the fact that a certain type of theory can be constructed around them. It is a real question, not to be settled by decree, whether, for example, modal and deontic logics can be incorporated with traditional logic into a single generalized logic. Conventionalism, if used to short-circuit such investigations, gives us not greater freedom of inquiry, but merely freedom *from* inquiry—a licence to retreat from criticism.

Naturally, we begin from a list—explicit or implicit—of what we take to be classes and what we take to be categories. But if we find no way of distinguishing them, this is as much as to say that the distinction is of no theoretical consequence. We may then modify the lists in what we expect to be a more promising way; there is a certain interplay between list-membership and the progress of our investigation. Quite arbitrarily to stand by the original lists is to cut clean across the established principles of inquiry. If we say that 'are' is, but 'greater than' is not, a logical constant; that 'disposition' is a category but that 'colour' is not; that 'my kangaroo is not a kangaroo' is logically false, but 'my kangaroo is the fifth day of the week' is empirically false, we have to justify these distinctions by showing, for example, that questions about whether something is coloured are settled in a quite different way from questions about whether 'brittle' is a dispositional predicate. And if it is not apparent that the way of settling *is* different, that, too, has to be argued. Thus, in the present instance, Ryle cannot avoid the question whether we can, and how we are to, distinguish between a false statement and an absurd sentence; for my part, I cannot avoid the question whether, and how, I can distinguish between a formal and an empirical consequence. To treat as a matter of decision the distinction between false and absurd, between formal and empirical, rather than the original distinction between class and category, would be arbitrariness of the second degree, arbitrariness about the point at which to be arbitrary. But the responsibility which is thus incumbent upon me, to give grounds for distinguishing between formal and empirical is too heavy, and would carry me too far from my present theme, to be embarked upon now; it will suffice for my present purpose if I have shown that it is in fact my responsibility, that conventionalism does not provide us with an easy escape route from philosophical reasoning.

For the rest, if moral be needed, Fowler has already supplied it in *Modern English Usage*: 'Category should be used by no one who is not prepared to state (1) that he does not mean *class* and (2) that he knows the difference between the two'. But what is it 'not to mean *class*'? And how are we to persuade others, or even ourselves, that 'we know the difference between the two'?

INDEX